Obliterating
Exceptionalism

Obliterating Exceptionalism

A chronicle of Obama's Politically Correct Progressive destruction of America

Kent Clizbe

For Normal Americans, clinging to guns and religion.

Ashburn, Virginia, USA
www.kentclizbe.com
kent@kentclizbe.com

10 9 8 7 6 5 4 3 2

Table of Contents

Part One

Domestic Obliteration

Obama, Osama, and Moammar

Chapter 18

John Brennan— Connecting the Dots Spells Conflict of Interest

Chapter 19

Maghreb Mutinies: Karl Marx Meet Sayid Qutb; Lenin Meet Osama bin Laden

Chapter 20

North Korea: President Obama, Time to Be a Leader

Part Three

Military Obliteration

Chapter 21

Libya: Obama's Progressively Flexible War

Big Peace, September 15, 2011

Chapter 22

War-time Priorities—Tilting at Lavender Windmills

Chapter 23

Negotiations with the Taliban—Foreign Affairs and Eggheads

Chapter 24

Ministry of Truth Declaration: Combat is Assistance

Part Four

Global War on Terror (uh, "contingency operations")

Chapter 25

"Good War" Counter-Insurgency R$_x$—Colonize or Come Home
Originally published:

Chapter 26

Counter-insurgency—Lessons from a Professional in the Philippines, Frontlines of the Global War on Terror

Epilogue

Tribute to an American Leader

Ronald Reagan—Inspiration for Personal Development

Chapter 1

Candidate Vetting Failure—Catastrophic Results

Originally appeared: NewsMax, March 28, 2011

As an executive recruiter, I provided a 100% guarantee to my clients. When I provided a company with a candidate for a job, that candidate was ready, willing and able to do the job. If the candidate quit or was fired in the first three months, I returned my fee. Never once did I have to repay a fee.

A successful placement of a high level professional, usually a double PhD, in return for a five figure placement fee, requires a multi-step process. However, the most crucial step is vetting the candidate. I spent hours talking to the candidate, assessing his motivations, expertise, and qualifications. The candidate provided references and signed releases to allow me to obtain records of his education, citizenship, criminal history, civil court actions, and other documents.

As a CIA case officer, I dealt with foreigners, some with dubious backgrounds, making outrageous claims, in search of solutions to their problems. I had to assess their personalities, motivations, and the basics of their story— were they who they said they were; did they have access to what they claimed? This process relied on my street smarts, people skills, and assessment abilities. Usually no documents were available for vetting. I was successful because I ran operations like a business—with results required.

More than once, I uncovered problems in existing cases. Agents lied to their case officers; some had been lying for years. In many cases, the case officer, trained and experienced, but not street smart, or in love with his agent, was not really interested in the truth. Continuing to run a bad asset has very few immediate or obvious downsides. Uncovering lies makes handling an asset much more difficult.

Meeting and developing a relationship with a potential espionage agent requires the same care as recruiting a computational linguist for a Silicon Valley start-up, but the stakes are much higher. Not in monetary terms, but for the security of our country. Lives are at stake.

Placing a candidate who lies about his education with a commercial client would damage both my pocketbook and my reputation. Recruiting an espionage agent who works for an enemy intelligence service could be deadly. Seven CIA employees paid with their lives in December 2010 when a "vetted" candidate killed himself and his CIA case officer in Afghanistan.

Assessing personalities and detecting deception are two skills that have been profitable—monetarily, and in fighting terrorists and enemies. Vetting and validation of candidates is a difficult and unrewarding process. But on-going vetting and validation of the bona fides of candidates is a must, if you are serious about your reputation, or the security of your country.

Vetting candidates for political office makes vetting espionage agents, or dot.com engineers, look like child's play. The damage a liar or enemy infiltrator can do to our country is potentially astronomical.

In the 2010 Congressional elections, I vetted a Tea Party candidate, without his cooperation. The issues I identified should have disqualified him. Besides lying about his degree, and exaggerating his work in the private sector, there were unanswered questions with the candidate's long record of military service. As is typical with those caught covering up the truth, the candidate went on the attack.

The stakes for vetting a candidate for President of the United States make any other kind of vetting work seem silly. If a liar, or faker, or cheat was to make it into the White House our constitutional system could be at risk.

In my experience, a valid candidate, with nothing to hide, is eager to help in the vetting process. From providing full details of his personal and professional background, to revealing deep personal issues, a valid candidate works with those doing the vetting.

In the 2008 Presidential election, candidates were vetted by the press in varying degrees. The media examined, analyzed and publicly evaluated them. John McCain's personal wealth, marriage, place of birth, mental stability, and other important issues. McCain cooperated, provided details and answered questions.

On the other hand, Barack Obama's background remains nearly a blank slate. His school records, from kindergarten to law school, remain hidden. The story of his financial support is hidden—his private elementary and high school in Hawaii, his international travel, his graduate and undergraduate tuition and living expenses, and more. And these are just the beginning of the Barack Obama vetting failure.

My extensive research into the espionage operations of the Communist International (Comintern), detailed in Willing Accomplices, familiarized me with their techniques. One of their most common tactics to respond to exposure is so pervasive that it could be their motto: Admit nothing. Deny everything. Make counter-accusations.

For a professional vetter, it is clear that one candidate in 2008 was concealing vital information, at best. The documents and stories floated to support the candidate's claims only raise more suspicion.

The most disturbing aspect of attempts to vet the mystery candidate was the Obama camp's vigorous response. Their stereotypical response is nearly as damning as any information that could be revealed: Admitting nothing, denying everything, and making counter-accusations, the vetting of candidate Obama continues.

Do we need a professional candidate vetter? It looks like the project may have just begun. The future of our country might depend on it.

Chapter 2
Obama's Worldview and the Roots Political Correctness: KGB Covert Influence Operations

Originally appeared in NewsMax; Sept. 30, 2008

In the 1920s, Vladimir Lenin charged a select group of communist espionage officers with a long range covert influence project. Their goal: To undermine the culture, society, and economy of the USA. To weaken America in preparation for a socialist revolution. The communists targeted the three transmission belts of American culture: Academia, the Media, and Hollywood. Recent research reveals the unbelievable extent of their success. Today we see the results in Obama's campaign talking points, the Media's assistance, and Hollywood and Academia's slavish toeing of the party line.

The communist ops were focused on the long term. The operators were convinced that political evolution had reached its high point in Russia. The revolution would spread across the globe. Their covert operators had long term horizons, measured in decades rather than months. Their leaders changed, Lenin to Stalin. KGB chiefs were regularly slaughtered, along with millions of other Soviet citizens. Yet the covert influence ops remained active from 1920 to the fall of Russian communism in 1980. Not even the most optimistic KGB minion dared dream their operations would echo into the 21st century.

In fact, the seeds planted by the Communist spies have grown into a kudzu plant that still sprouts new shoots, spreading its noxious tendrils throughout the USA, thriving even as the gardeners that planted them are long dead.

Communist intelligence officers infiltrated the cultural transmission belts of American society and planted covert influence payloads. Comparing the content of the original payloads to today's PC creed reveals them to be identical.

The payload and methodology was best summarized by a communist agent working against Hollywood, quoted by Stephen Koch:

"You claim to be an independent-minded idealist. You don't really understand politics, but you think the little guy is getting a lousy break.

You believe in open-mindedness. You are shocked, frightened by what is going on right here in our own country. You're frightened by the racism, by the oppression of the workingman. You think the Russians are trying a great human experiment, and you hope it works. You believe in peace.

You yearn for international understanding. You hate fascism.

You think the capitalist system is corrupt. You say it over and over and over again." [1]

One of the first, and certainly most effective, recruitments for the covert influence program was the New York Times' Walter Duranty. Recently completed analysis, in conjunction with former KGB operators, of Duranty's lifestyle, access, and reporting reveals that he was, almost without doubt, a paid espionage agent. Duranty, America's man in Moscow for more than a decade supplied the US media with a steady stream of communist-fed information. The implied subtext of Duranty's message was: "Communism works. It is inevitable. The USA is doomed" KGB operators now admit that they were tasked to continue implanting such messages up until the fall of the USSR. [2]

The media accepted Duranty's covert influence messages as gospel. He won the Pulitzer Prize in 1932. The KGB must have gloated over their unbelievable success. Duranty, and the New York Times, set the template for America's press to be manipulated by the KGB. He was "the doyenne of left-leaning Westerners who believe that what happened inside Soviet Russia held the key to the future for the rest of the world." 3

The Soviet-trained intelligence service of North Vietnam infiltrated the American press corps in Saigon, another covert influence coup. Pham Xuan An, a communist espionage agent, worked for Time magazine for almost 30 years. Beginning as a translator, he ended his career as the last Time correspondent in Saigon, filing stories for publication in the US after the North Vietnamese victory. All the while, An was a communist espionage agent. Morley Safer, upon An's death in 2006, evidently without irony, called him one of the "best-connected journalists in the country." 4

In 1934, the operation against America's Education system bore fruit at the Teachers College of Columbia University. A group of intellectuals began their contribution to the communist project to destroy traditional American society, calling themselves, "Reconstructionists." Their message planned for every classroom, called for educators to be "less frightened of imposition and indoctrination." 5

My analysis reveals that the leader of this group, George Counts, was likely a covert influence agent. His multiple trips to the USSR, from the late 1920s to the early '30s, place him squarely in the sights of the KGB's covert influence operators. During his travels across the communist country, he would have been squired by intelligence officers, who would develop him for eventual recruitment. The success of this covert influence recruitment is reflected in Counts' books, published in 1931, The New Russian Primer, and The Soviet Challenge to America. The first was a direct translation of a communist indoctrination text for Soviet children, extolling the virtues of the first Five Year Plan. His co-author was a Soviet "translator," most likely supplied by the KGB.

Covert ops against American schools were in full swing by 1937. Agents of covert influence working as teachers in elementary and secondary schools carried out their indoctrination "without exposing themselves." Their covert influence mission was to "affect the children's thinking, and ...mobilize other teachers." 6

According to PC in 2008, the United States is a racist, sexist, classist, homophobic, bigoted, war-mongering fascist imperialist State. What we think of as a "Politically Correct" point of view, is the Leninist/Stalinist covert influence payload, emerged from underground.

When the kudzu pushed up from its underground hiatus after the 60's, Bill Ayers and Obama's foundation in Chicago pushed for school reform. Ayers said, "Teachers should be community organizers dedicated to provoking resistance to American racism and oppression. His preferred alternative? 'I'm a radical, Leftist, small 'c' communist,'"7 The covert operation bears fruit decades later.

Willi Muenzenberg, Lenin's chief covert influence operator was determined to instill the mindset in Americans that, as Koch says, "to criticize or challenge Soviet policy was the unfailing mark of a bad, bigoted, and probably stupid person, while support was equally infallible proof of a forward-looking mind committed to all that was best for humanity and marked by an uplifting refinement of sensibility." 8 This is as close as we can come to a definition of PC today. Simply substitute "Soviet" with "Democrat," or "Liberal," and there you have it. Keith Olbermann could not express the PC point of view any more clearly. The covert influence payload emerges today as PC.

Muenzenberg's operations, run from Vienna and Paris, dispatched communist espionage officers into Hollywood. There they built solid operations, recruiting screenwriters, producers, actors, directors, and hangers-on. Their success against the film industry was notable and unparalleled. Underground, and overt communist organizations flourished there. One communist recruit explained how the party made him comfortable: "I would be spared the agony of thinking my way through difficult issues: all the thinking would be done for me by an elite core of trained cerebrators..."9

The Hollywood strategy was wildly successful over the long-term. The elite corps of today, Michael Moore, Barbra Streisand, Matt Damon, Oliver Stone, et al, saves the PC multitudes from doing any heavy thinking. The elites provide emotionally satisfying, Politically Correct views on any and all issues, packaged for the consumption of the PC proletariat.

When Obama recently decried the bitterness of Midwesterners clinging to their guns, their religion and their anti-immigrant sentiments, he was echoing the Leninist/Stalinist covert payload of decades ago. When Obama's preacher, Mr. Wright, accused the US government of inflicting AIDS on "people of color," as a means of genocide, he parroted a KGB covert influence operational payload, first inserted in an Indian paper in 1984. 10

When Progressives today chant, "Bush lied, people died," they parrot the KGB's messages. In the run-up to World War II, the communists characterized President Roosevelt as a war-mongering imperialist, and American foreign policy as somehow evil, and definitely naive. Reading the comments on virtually any Daily Kos posting today reveals the astounding success of the KGB's influence op.

The goals of PC, which began to emerge after the 1970s, up until today, are nearly identical to the goals of the Communist International in 1920: Destroy the society in which capitalism thrives. Bring the capitalists to their knees, so that the Elite Vanguard can install a dictatorship of the proletariat, for the good of all mankind. The proletariat is too gullible and easily swayed by logic and reality. The Elites know better than the masses.

The Leninist Elite Vanguard of the Proletariat in 1920 is today's Elite Vanguard of Progressives, with Obama as the public face. They know better than you. They are oh-so-smart, oh-so-cosmopolitan, oh-so-loved in Vienna and Paris. They plan to give the rubes and hayseeds of fly-over country what's best for them, like it or not, made palatable by oratory and lies, and spoon-fed by their friends in the media, Hollywood, and academia.

Only difference between then and now is: Now we know better. Don't be fooled again.

Notes

1 Double Lives, 2004, pp. 249-250.

2 Interviews with former KGB case officers, Washington DC, 2008.

3 Taylor, S.J. Stalin's Apologist: Walter Duranty: The New York Times's Man in   Moscow., 1990, p. 5.

4 Safer, Flashbacks: On Returning to Vietnam, 1990.

5 Ravitch, The Troubled Crusade, 1980, p. 85.

6 Budenz, The Techniques of Communism, 1954, p. 209.

7 "Obama and Ayers Pushed Radicalism in Schools," Wall St Journal, September 23, 2008, p. A28.

8 Double Lives, 2004, p. 15.

9 Radosh, Ronald, and Allis Radosh. Red Star over Hollywood: The Film Colony's Long Romance with the Left, 2006, p. 43.

10 Andrew & Mitrokhin, The World was Going Our Way, 2005, p. 340.

Chapter 3
The Holder/Obama GWCIA

Originally published in NewsMax; Aug. 31, 2009

In the early days and weeks after September 11, 2001, a small cadre of men (and a few women) with vast amounts of intelligence experience reported to the Langley, Virginia headquarters of the CIA. These unsung heroes were then dispatched across the globe to run operations against the Al-Qaeda conspirators who leveled the World Trade Center and struck our mighty military's nerve center.

The FBI, a domestic law enforcement agency, did not have the ability or skills needed to track down and strike the attackers overseas. The Pentagon, with F22s, nuclear aircraft carriers, intercontinental ballistic missiles, and battalions of the best armor in the history of mankind, was like an elephant attacked by a mouse—mighty, but helpless in its mammoth rage.

Our best hope lay with the grey-bearded intelligence professionals who fanned out across the world. Supplementing the skeleton crew of staff officers left in the wake of the Clintons' anti-intelligence scourging of the CIA, the volunteers went to the Middle East, Asia, Europe, Africa, South America, to the most remote and isolated outposts in the world. Sometimes they worked with friendly forces, and sometimes they worked alone. They focused like a laser beam on one thing—protect our country. Stop the next attack. Seek and destroy the terrorist planners, facilitators, trainers, financiers, and their infrastructure wherever they were.

Twenty-four hours a day, seven days a week, CIA officers, both the contractors and the over-extended staff officers, launched dozens of initiatives. The Counter-terrorist Center's motto, "Deny, Disrupt, Destroy," became the reason for our living. We left our families for months on end and sacrificed personal and professional lives to fight the Global War on Terror. Google "Jihadists in Paradise," for an unauthorized account of one of my contributions (which I have been advised that I can neither confirm nor deny).

As I did my part in the Middle East, Southeast Asia, and Africa, my family tried to maintain a semblance of normalcy at home. My son was in eighth grade in September 2001. I did not see him graduate that year. I was home less than six months for each of the first three of his high school years. Even with nightly phone calls, his grades and attitude plummeted in my absence. He went from a happy, engaged, charming 13 year old with straight A's and a focus on the future, to a sullen, uncommunicative, high school flunky. I put my successful and lucrative executive recruiting business on hold for eight years. Finally, after five years of patriotic sacrifices, my family sacrifice account was overdrawn. Coming home was an option for me, and I took it.

Others did not take that option, and they sacrificed the quality of their marriages, participation in their children's and grandchildren's lives, the profitability of their businesses, and more. Personal and professional issues festered and rotted while they fought to keep America safe and prevented further attacks on our homeland.

In contrast, where was Eric Holder? Before leaving President Clinton's employ, he orchestrated the pardons of several Puerto Rican separatist terrorists. Then in 2003, as a partner in the Washington law firm of Covington & Burling, Mr. Holder's client, Chiquita Brands, admitted paying to support terrorist death squads in Columbia and paid a $25 million fine. During the time that my friends worked to disrupt and destroy terrorist networks

threatening America, Holder's firm represented
- 16 terrorist detainees held at Guantanamo.

Did he make any personal or professional sac
his country was attacked in 2001? If he has, it is
find. When the Special Prosecutor comes call
someone from Covington & Burling can represent my
colleagues for free, like they did for Lakhdar Boumedienne
and ten other terrorists in Gitmo.

The Holder/Obama Global War on the CIA (GWCIA) has
only just begun, as it debuted with "grisly revelations" of
revving drills, gunshots in the next cell, and threats against
a terrorist's children. The GWOT is not for the faint of
heart, nor the queasy. No war ever has been. There may
be slight improprieties stashed in the CIA's closets, but the
liberal-appeasing GWCIA is foolhardy and dangerous.

Mike Spann, was the first to die in the GWOT. He won't
have to worry about the Holder/Obama GWCIA. But
others in the Agency are very worried. While we sacrificed
to achieve incremental victories, Holder and Obama
plotted and schemed -- not against those "evil-mongers"
who killed our countrymen, but against those of us hunting
the terrorists. Something is rotten in the state of Denmark.
The odor is not from Langley, Mr. Holder.

Chapter 4
SOTUS 2011—WTF?!

Originally appeared in: BigPeace, Jan. 27, 2011

Barack Obama's handlers and speech writers revealed their re-election strategy last night in his State of the Union speech. The Obama clique thinks they are replicating Slick Willy Clinton's (and Dick Morris's) triangulation strategy after the electoral Waterloo in 1994.

Maybe they need Rahm Emanuel back in the White House. They need somebody with a clue.

Instead of Clinton's sharp tack to the right, the Obama clique has replicated Gerald Ford's muddled economic/political strategy: Whip Inflation Now! (WIN).

Unfortunately (for Obama and his clueless handlers), they forgot to check out the acronym for their apparent campaign slogan for 2012: Obama 2012—Win the Future! (WTF).

The commander in chief used the phrase, or a variation of it, about ten times in his speech last night. Clearly they have decided to replace "Hope, Change, Believe," and "Yes, We Can" with "WTF." Good luck with that, Barack.

It took my 15 year old 2 seconds to crack up, after I pointed out the acronym—as he texted his way through watching the SOTUS with me. WTF? For non-texters, WTF is texting shorthand for "What the F***?"

Here are a few of the WTF lines from our fearless leader's speech:

Green energy? WTF!

More government "investments"? WTF!

Sputnik? WTF!

Solar shingles? WTF!

"Sunlight and water" fuel? WTF!

Gang wars at school? WTF!

Illegal aliens pledging allegiance to the American flag? WTF!

Give 80% of Americans access to high-speed rail? WTF!

Avoid TSA pat-downs, take the train? WTF!

A flaw in Obamacare? WTF!

Obama will make sure we're not "buried under a mountain of debt?" WTF!

Repealing ObamaCare will add "a quarter trillion dollars to our deficit?" WTF!

Raising taxes on "millionaires" to "promote America's success?" WTF!

Give Americans a government that is more competent and more efficient?" WTF!

Ensure that "special interests are not larding up legislation with pet projects?" WTF!

He has "renewed" and "restored" America's standing in the world? WTF!

Thanks to Obama's geniuses, we now have the perfect re-election slogan: Obama 2012—WTF?!

Chapter 5
Exposing Kagan's Socialist Roots

May 2010

Elena Kagan's love affair with Socialism is not new, nor is it unique, in academia. Her credentials, like those of President Obama, are tethered to a common Progressive worldview. Harvard, Columbia University, the University of Chicago, Yale, all show up in the pedigrees of Progressive "change" agents, and community organizers. Bill Ayers, Kagan, Obama, and other Progressives, all advocate a radical restructuring of American culture and society. The shocking truth is that the Progressive, anti-American worldview did not arise by itself in these liberal enclaves.

Research has documented extensively the USSR's intelligence operations in the United States. From the birth of the Soviet communist state, until the McCarthy era, the KGB and its predecessors actively carried out phenomenally successful covert operations throughout the US.

Publication of the Venona Files, and Mitrokhin's cache of KGB documents, confirmed that the KGB had successfully penetrated both the US government, and private organizations. KGB tradecraft, recruiting techniques, and communications plans are familiar to an intelligence professional of today. Their intelligence collection operations have been analyzed extensively.

What has not been analyzed previously is the extent of the KGB's covert influence operations. My recent counter-intelligence analysis of selected targets revealed the KGB's successes. In fact, the communist covert influence operations had a greater and longer lasting impact on America than did their better known intelligence gathering operations. Covert influence is a much finer and more insidious instrument of covert action than its cousin, propaganda. Covert influence operations slip messages into classrooms, articles and movies.

The KGB focused their covert influence operations on the institutions that were the traditional keepers of American culture—the media (newspapers), education and academia, and entertainment (Hollywood). They enjoyed great success in all three domains.

The message, first articulated and implanted by the Communist International's covert influence master, Willi Muenzenberg, was simple: "America is a racist, sexist, xenophobic, nation of haters, built on the backs of slaves. Communism is a noble experiment." Notice the similarities to today's Political Correctness (PC). The messages are exactly the same, and are like strands of DNA, revealing the genetic roots of today's PC.

For now, let's focus on Elena Kagan's domain—academia. Communist intelligence operatives, very soon after their stunning success in Russia, targeted American academia. Let's compare the response of an Ivy League college to an unpopular American war (World War I), to Kagan's response to a wildly popular American war (the War on Terror).

Prior to the Russian revolution, American academia was a champion of fundamental American values—freedom, liberty, capitalism, patriotism. In the run-up to America's entry into World War I (WWI), Yale students and faculty formed a military training club. They drilled and prepared themselves for war. In March 1917, academia and media joined in calling for patriotism and service to America. A New York Times journalist, and the President of Yale, spoke at Yale's student newspaper anniversary dinner. The President lauded the campus newspaper's call for student military training. The Times reporter told the Yale students that they all owed a duty to the Government. He advocated compulsory military duty, in return for their "enjoying government protection." He went on to say that when the call came to serve in the military, "We will all be Americans...You will respond to the call of the Government in...the great Yale traditions."

Fast forward to 2003, Elena Kagan, dean of Harvard Law School, in the middle of a global war in which Americans were fighting and dying, was in "deep distress" because the American military was allowed to meet with prospective recruits on campus. Then, before the Supreme Court reversed, by a 9-0 decision, an appellate court's ruling that supported her stand, Kagan banned American military recruiters from using Harvard Law's placement office.

The stark difference between the pre-communist-covert-influence response in 1917 and Kagan's oh-so-PC response in 2003 is stunning. Recent research has revealed the extent to which American media and American academia were penetrated by Soviet covert influence operations, beginning soon after WWI. A side-by-side comparison of the attitudes towards America's involvement in military actions, 1917 with 2003, stuns any objective observer.

Kagan is helpless to be anything but an anti-American, socialist stooge. She is a product of an academic system that is permeated by the anti-American message, for nearly 100 years. To move up in American academia, one must be a PC true believers. The covert influence message planted by communists carries on like an advertising campaign that never quits. After the anti-American messages were planted by agents of influence in American media, academia, and Hollywood, the KGB's officers were mostly annihilated in purges. But the messages, like an advertising jingle stuck in your head, echo through the ivy halls, up till today.

So, when Kagan's stands on various issues, including her banning American military recruiters from her socialist campus redoubt, are considered as she is vetted for the Supreme Court, remember where her attitudes and beliefs come from. By understanding the origin of her PC worldview, we can, and must, be clear that we reject her anti-American beliefs, and the roots of her beliefs.

Chapter 6
Boxer's Response to ClimateGate— Admit Nothing, Deny Everything, Make Counter-accusations

ParcBench, *December 3, 2009*

Earlier this week, Sen. Barbara Boxer, California Democrat, during her committee's hearings on "Climate Change," shared her view of the recent whistleblower revelations about "Global Warming." The release of smoking gun emails between the high priests of the Anthropogenic Global Warming (AGW) cult, as well as computer code used to "model" climate variables, has been hailed as a revelation of staggering proportions by concerned citizens, scientists, and taxpayers around the world.

However, Ms Boxer's attitude towards whistleblowers is much less welcoming than one might expect. Imagine if a whistleblower in the Bush White House had released emails documenting Karl Rove's admonition to Colin Powell to "hide the results" showing that there were no nukes in Saddam's Iraq. She may have had a different attitude toward that whistleblower than the harsh feelings she has for the mole in the British university.

Ms Boxer emphasized that her interest in exploring the ClimateGate issue was not to get to the bottom of faked science, paid for with US taxpayer dollars. No, Senator Boxer, wants to call it "Email-theft-gate," and she wants to look into potentially coordinated "criminal activity" involved in the release of the smoking gun code and emails.

As this slow motion train wreck unfolds for our viewing pleasure (the exquisite timing of the release—with President Obama scheduled to declare a continued lowering of the sea level in Copenhagen within days—is delicious), we must continue to monitor the opposition, and be prepared for their tactics and methods of operation.

In our upcoming project, Brett Joshpe and I will share detailed accounts of how Progressives/Liberals/Democrats (choose your term based on the staleness of their last title) in America operate in the trenches, and why. My background as a CIA operations officer allowed me to understand deeply the power of what is known in the espionage trade as "Covert Influence" operations.

International communists were masters of Covert Influence, and zeroed in on the three institutions that controlled the transmission of America's cultural heritage—the Media, Education/Academia, and Hollywood. They realized that they would never be able to destroy America by military might alone. Masters of subterfuge and covert influence during the Russian Revolution, the communists turned their attention to their new enemies around 1920. Their covert influence strategy was just like advertising. Insert subtle messages into multiple delivery vehicles, never being too blatant. The common theme of the payloads could be summed up as "America is an irredeemably greedy, racist, foreigner-hating, fascist country."

Recruiting "Willing Accomplices" in the press, universities and education, and in Hollywood was surprisingly easy. Many Americans were ripe for the picking, and served quietly and efficiently in their influence roles. Careful counter-intelligence research has revealed identities of agents of influence in all three spheres of American life. The payload insertion began in the 1920s, and continued unabated through the salad days of communist espionage, right through World War II.

When KGB professionals were recalled to Moscow and summarily executed during Stalin's purges, their replacements were unable to renew their covert influence networks. This was not a problem, however. The American Willing Accomplices had already imbibed the payloads, the attitude, and the methods and techniques of covert influence operations. They simply continued operating, on their own.

After WWII, the communists were on the run. Espionage conspiracies were exposed by former comrades who defected to the side of freedom. The FBI investigated many operatives. Other counter-intelligence work by American and allied services revealed multiple penetrations throughout the government and other institutions. With communist penetration of American institutions being exposed almost daily, agents fully exercised their KGB training.

A fundamental response to exposure of covert action operations is boiled down to a motto, well-known to covert action operatives. In case of exposure or questioning by authorities: Admit nothing. Deny everything. Make counter-accusations. This was the technique honed in revolution, proven in wartime, and adopted by American agents of influence.

Again and again, the Willing Accomplices employed this tactic. The Rosenbergs. Alger Hiss. The "Hollywood Ten." Those correctly accused of having communist connections used this technique to perfection. The beauty of this technique is that it works. Alger Hiss was still being defended by Progressives well into the 21st century, long past any doubt of his true guilt. Joseph McCarthy, although he was right in the substance of his accusations of communist penetration of the bulwarks of American government, was successfully vilified with counter-accusations until his name became an epithet.

The Willing Accomplices in the media, academia, and Hollywood ran cover for their comrades. As the 50s matured into the 60s, the template of reaction became boilerplate. And the payload matured into the mantras of today's Political Correctness: "America is a mean-spirited, hateful, fascist, racist, sexist, xenophobic, hating country built on the backs of the oppressed and minorities."

This digression into ancient history is necessary in discussing Sen. Boxer's counter-accusations because it better helps us to understand the pedigree of Sen. Boxer's tactics. Tried and true, her tactics were taught to the original Willing Accomplices by the communist covert operators. Decades of practice has honed the Progressives' response to exposure of the dirty truths of their ideology (like the ClimateGate emails). With animal cunning instincts, they admit nothing, deny everything, and make counter-accusations.

And their allies in the institutions penetrated by the influence operations provide cover and justification for whatever the Progressives do, regardless of right or wrong.

One last note with regards to the AGW issue and its historical foundation. The advocates for massive reductions of energy use in America are quite simply acting on the KGB's covert influence payloads. Once the message sank in, after repetitions throughout our culture—in elementary school (Recycling is Fun! Do it or the earth will explode.), in college (We are killing Gaia by driving cars.), in the media (Al Gore is our savior), and Hollywood (Inconvenient Truth slide show wins an Oscar!)—the American public was nearly powerless to resist the nearly irresistible conclusion of decades of covert influence messages. "America must be punished before it can do further harm to the Earth."

With this background in mind, now is the time to finally stand and say "Ms Boxer, have you no shame? Enough is enough, ma'm." While there are many websites and blogs commenting on this issue, it is time for take a page from the President's playbook—let's organize our community for action.

Chapter 7
Covert Influence—Russian Operations Changed America

Originally published as a serial in: BigPeace, July 31, August 1, and August 2, 2010

This June the FBI arrested a group of Russian intelligence officers and agents. American commentators were puzzled at the spies' lack of success in stealing "secrets." Even though the KGB has enjoyed great success in covert influence operations against the culture of the United States throughout the last hundred years, most Americans are still largely blind to the 20th century's "great game," the war against America that communists won.

Federal prosecutors brought the Russian spies to court several days after their arrest. Vicky Pelaez, a Spanish-language writer for an American media service, was a pitiful sight. She appeared dazed and confused, a Hispanic housewife snatched from her kitchen.

Vicky Pelaez

Dazzled by Jason Bourne and Jack Bauer, and ignorant of the most effective forms of espionage, Americans didn't know what to make of the pudgy Peruvian-born journalist. Seemingly, the main concern the media was the plight of her children. The Huffington Post speculated that she was betrayed by her handling officer—her husband. Many Americans were distracted by the slutty daughter of a KGB officer, caught peddling her wares as a swallow (KGB's term for the bait in sex-traps). Little did Americans realize that the frumpy journalist, Vicky Pelaez, was the latest warrior in a century-long, vicious attack on America. The sex-kitten was just a shiny bauble to distract us.

In the early days of the struggle for world domination between the USA and global communism, American statesmen were clueless about the enemy they faced. They were clueless about the rules of the struggle. They were ignorant of the communists' tactics. And they arrogantly refused to learn.

In 1929, more than a decade after the Bolsheviks had imposed communism on Russia, the American Secretary of State, Henry Stimson, politely declined to take part in espionage, averring that, "Gentlemen don't read each other's mail."

The Bolsheviks, however, were not gentlemen. In 1929, the Russians were already reading our mail, even as we refused the offer to read others'. The communists had, so to speak, slipped into our house at night and were living in our basement. The communists were playing a game that America had never understood. Even at that early date, they were winning. Their strategy: covert influence operations.

Intel Collection vs. Active Measures

There are two major types of espionage operations: intelligence collection, and, in the KGB's terminology, active measures. Intelligence collection is stealing secrets. The Rosenbergs were Soviet espionage agents focused on stealing and reporting America's nuclear secrets.

Collection operations are fragile and perishable. The success of the operation, and its life-span, depends on the agent's access to secrets, his willingness to continue stealing secrets, and his ability to avoid detection. Loss of access, change in motivation, or detection by authorities bring the operation to an immediate end. When the Rosenberg op was disrupted, there was no more product, no more secrets—it died with the communist agents in the electric chair.

Active measures arose from the communists' long fight against the tsar. Outlawed as a party, the communists organized covert cells. Without strong military capabilities, they learned how to use the tools of active measures—propaganda, disinformation, and agents of influence—against the royal government.

Early American Flirtation with Active Measures

Partly in response to the communist revolution, Woodrow Wilson's Progressive administration tried its hand at overt propaganda. In April, 1917, Wilson formed America's first 20th century propaganda group—the Committee on Public Information (CPI). The CPI's main objective was to bring the US into WWI, and to weaken German power. The CPI's targets were both domestic and international. Among the international targets was Russia. Conflicting objectives created confusion, however. The Bolshevik threat to American business interests in Russia was of concern, but a strong communist Russia was also a powerful deterrent to German power. The CPI was disbanded after operating for two years. The effort left a bad taste in Washington's mouth, but created some native expertise.

Poster for CPI Propaganda Movie

After Wilson's short-lived stab at the influence game, it was only after World War II that America began to understand the rules of the game. When we belatedly tried to play, it was too late. The Russians had the upper hand. The KGB and its predecessors had infiltrated and begun the process of twisting to their benefit the most intimate domains of our culture.

Lenin Initiates Covert Influence Operations

Flush with success and certain of global communist domination, in 1921 Vladimir Lenin surveyed the situation. His army was all but imaginary. Worn down by WWI and the internal wars that followed, the Russian military was no match for any of its neighbors. Prosecuting a shooting war in Europe, Asia, or America was beyond the possible for the Red Army.

At the same time, Lenin was having second thoughts about Marxist dogma. The whole "dictatorship of the proletariat" theory looked ridiculous in the cold light of reality. He announced variations on communist theory, producing what became known as Marxism-Leninism. The key rationalization was that dictatorship by the masses was a goal, maybe a long-term goal. In the meantime, before reaching this paradise, Russia and humanity would go through a transition.

Lenin's theory explained that during the early phases after establishing a communist state, an "Elite Vanguard" would control all decision-making, while preparing the masses for full communism. Russian elites, Lenin's communist cronies, were the vanguard. With this justification of his dictatorship, Lenin provided a template for intellectuals to embrace his ideology. The need for an Elite made them special, and necessary, and gave them great power. At the same time they could claim to be wielding power "for the little people, the masses."

ComIntern for Covert Influence

Faced with his lack of military strength, Lenin conceived a plan for global spread of communism using his party's proven covert capabilities. He established the Communist International (ComIntern). This ostensibly independent group of communist leaders from around the globe was actually a front for Soviet political control. It also provided cover for international intelligence operations. After Stalin seized the reins of Soviet power, he strengthened the covert ops begun by Lenin, even as he ruthlessly murdered many of the operators. Though he did away with the ComIntern, its intelligence operations continued.

Covert Influence Methodology

The most long-lasting, virulent, and dangerous active measure is covert influence. In a covert influence operation a payload is secretly inserted into some part of the enemy's communications channels. The ultimate goal of covert influence is to transform the enemy in a way that is useful to the attacker.

In a typical covert influence operation an intelligence officer targets an agent of influence. The target is chosen for access to a desired channel of communications (the ComIntern intel operators targeted American media, academia, and Hollywood). The intelligence officer uses standard recruiting tradecraft to become friends with the targeted agent of influence. Appealing to the identified vulnerabilities of the targeted agent, the officer burrows into the target's life.

The targeted agent of influence may, or may not, know that she is dealing with a hostile intelligence service, even after she is recruited. The agent might provide her services because she believes in the message, or she may work for pay, or maybe for some other gratification. In the actual operation, the espionage officer provides the recruited agent of influence with the payload. The agent of influence inserts the payload into his communications channel. Once the payload is inserted, in the form of a news story, an editorial, a speech, a book, a lecture, a movie, a radio program, a song, a play, or any other form of communication, the payload takes on a life of its own.

The message can influence consumers for the rest of their lives. All it takes is one time exposure, and consumers' beliefs and attitudes can be changed. Reading a book or an article, hearing a song or a radio show, seeing a movie or a play are potentially life-changing experiences. The communist covert influence message was intended to change individual and societal morals and values.

In the Russians' Pelaez case, the intelligence officer's development and recruitment of the targeted journalist included marriage. This is a level of commitment and dedication that very few free world intelligence services can demand or expect. A steamy combination of true belief in her message, infatuation with her recruiting officer, substantial lifestyle benefits (a free ride to New York City and US citizenship) seemed to motivate Pelaez. Her influence work at the Hispanic newspaper in New York is typical of covert influence payloads. She denigrated the US and its policies, at the same time she lauded Latin American dictators, with the payload masked as her "point of view." It is likely that her influence work changed the attitudes and beliefs of hundreds or thousands of those exposed to her intel operations.

Covert Influence Not Propaganda
In covert influence, the payload is subtle. When done correctly, it is hard to identify the payload as anything but the creator's point of view. The payload is disguised as critical thinking, cultural criticism, or intellectual

theorizing. ~~Covert influence is not propaganda.~~ A propaganda message might be: "Imperialist America murders babies in Iraq!" A covert influence payload might be a movie that sensationalizes an incident on the battlefield, with an unspoken theme of American military complicity in war crimes. This insidious form of espionage is more difficult to identify than propaganda.

Willi Muenzenberg: Master of Influence Operations

The early USSR's intelligence services perfected covert influence. Their desired goal: destroy the will of the capitalist enemy to resist "inevitable" communist domination.

Willi Muenzenberg, 1920's

Working under the Communist International (ComIntern), Willi Muenzenberg, directed global covert influence operations, likely at Lenin's direction. A ComIntern press agent, publisher, movie maker, and middleman, German communist and long-time friend of Lenin, Willi was the mastermind behind Soviet intelligence's covert influence operations.

Muenzenberg's covert influence message was attractive to American intellectuals. The objective of the operations was to bring America down, sooner rather than later, so that communism could replace America's free enterprise and individualism with a dictatorship of Elites, and collectivism. Until his neck was broken by a rope in a French forest as Paris was captured from the Nazis in WWII, Muenzenberg honed his message to a fine point. His operational genius provided a message that seduced the intellectuals, without leaving any trace of Soviet involvement.

Willing Accomplices

Muenzenberg perfected the "Popular Front" operational concept. He and his agents set up multiple organizations with high-minded names and reasons for existence—for example the International Congress Against Fascism and War, and the Hollywood Anti-Nazi League. These fronts gave intellectuals and artists a higher calling—while serving as cover to insert covert influence payloads into the targeted cultures. The perceived moral superiority of the Soviet's covert influence messages provided members a chance to show "you were a decent human being," in fact, a better human being. Muenzenberg despised these members, and called them "Innocents."

I call these Americans "Willing Accomplices." They were witting, and unwitting, agents of influence. They were Willing to imbibe the superior attitude conferred by the high-minded ideals of the fronts. And they were Accomplices to the communists' goal of destroying their country.

Targets: American Media, Academia/Education, and Hollywood

Muenzenberg and his men, and later the KGB's ops officers in the US, targeted the most efficient conduits to influence American culture. The press, education and academia, and Hollywood were the fertile recruiting grounds of Muenzenberg's influence operations.

The payload was a simple formulation. Stephen Koch, for his book on Muenzenberg, "Double Lives," interviewed Willi's wife, Babette Gross, who survived the war to live into her 90s. Ms. Gross told Koch that Willi had carefully crafted the "payload" for his covert influence operations:

Reduced to its essence the message was: "You claim to be an independent-minded idealist. You don't really understand politics, but you think the little guy is getting a lousy break. You believe in open-mindedness. You are shocked, frightened by what is going on right here in our own country. You're frightened by the racism, by the oppression of the workingman. You believe in peace. You yearn for international understanding. You hate fascism. You think the capitalist system is corrupt."

This subtly anti-American message created a mindset. The mindset created a superiority complex among those who adopted it. They were smarter, better, more feeling, more caring, more humane, more human, overall better people than the unwashed masses. As Stephen Koch explained, "The purpose ... [was] to instill a reflexive loathing of the United States and its people as a prime tropism of left-wing enlightenment."

The attitude of wise superiority to the American masses, disdain for the racist, sexist, homophobic, foreigner-hating, dead-white-male-worshipping ignoramuses spread quickly throughout the three domains of cultural transmission. First academia rejected traditional America, her people, her founders, and her foundations. The press was next, closely followed by Hollywood.

The most stunning aspect of Muenzenberg's message was its ability to self-propagate. Like a fertile flower, once planted and growing, it spread its seeds far and wide, with no need for a gardener to nurture it. The payload, so powerful and seductive, once planted in the American intelligentsia, grew and metastasized, like a political cancer, until it burst forth in full flower as Political Correctness (PC) in the 1980s.

Muenzenberg's skillful covert influence operations, aiming to destroy American Exceptionalism, are still bearing fruit today. Willi's influence operations outlived every one of the ComIntern officers that recruited the Willing Accomplices, the American agents who carried the influence messages into the heart of our culture. The effects of Willi's operations outlived even the USSR, and even communism as a practical political platform.

Political Correctness 2010: Reflexive Loathing of the United States

It is not likely that any of the ComIntern covert influence operators realized that they were creating a monster that would grow for decades. They likely believed that after a few years their ops would have sown enough confusion to cause the global communist revolution they knew was coming. Even though the revolution never came in their lifetimes, the "hate America first" attitude slowly caught on. The Elites spread their anti-American message. It had to go underground from the late 1940s to the early 1960s. But after the late 1960s, the Elite Vanguard emerged in full flower.

A more concise description of Political Correctness cannot be found than Koch's formulation of Muenzenberg's covert influence payload. Look inside any PC ideas, speech codes, or requirements, and you'll find a "reflexive loathing" of traditional America, our values, history, and morals.

By the late 1980s, full-blown PC infected academia, education, the media, Hollywood, and American society in general. Americans were constantly bombarded with reminders of their hatefulness, bigotry, racism, sexism, and imperialism. Confused by the message of hate and disgust, while their daily lives were filled with positive energy, normal Americans became wracked with guilt. They were reminded daily that they were guilty of slavery, bigotry, killing babies in Vietnam, oppressing minorities and women around the globe, stealing the continent from the Indians, being arrogant in dealing with foreigners, killing the Earth with their hairspray, and various other sins.

In 2008, PC blossomed into full flower. In a spasm of PC-induced guilt, America elected our first anti-American president, who did not hide his disgust for normal Americans. Obama is the first president to apologize repeatedly for America's sins against foreign countries, and to speak disparagingly against the country that elected him. Obama's cool, detached Elite attitude, loathing the "bitter clingers" of the heartland, is a living testament to the power and success of Muenzenberg's covert influence operations.

Covert Influence Counter-measures

So, when American media seem to be puzzled as to the efficiency of Russian espionage operations against the US, and ignore the Russians' use of Pelaez as a covert influence operative, it is not surprising to a knowledgeable observer. The KGB's successors, the Russian Federation's intelligence service, learned all they know from the KGB. They have a long and successful history of working against America. They know the power of influence operations. The KGB, including Vladimir Putin has seen their influence ops succeed. The sorry state of PC-America is a direct result of Putin's predecessors' operations. All Americans should understand the power of past influence ops, and the potential for future influence ops.

Chapter 8
Russian Spy Ring: Covert Influence Continued

June 2010

Russian espionage professionals (let's just call them the KGB, their name of the moment doesn't matter) never quit targeting America. They infiltrated American society and planted the seeds of political correctness nearly one hundred years ago. Vladimir Putin is a KGB operations officer, and always will be. Manipulation and deception are as Russian as babushkas and vodka. The FBI's arrests this week of KGB operatives in America is not surprising. Neither is it surprising that their target seemed to be influence instead of intelligence gathering. One of the agents worked as a journalist.

The KGB was an evolutionary outgrowth of the tsar's own intelligence service.

Communism's collapse only pressed the pause button on the KBG's ops machine. A brief moment of openness and cooperation passed in the blink of an eye. Open archives slammed shut. Floods of revelations dried quickly. Cooperating offices became uncooperative.

After 2008, smelling weakness and sensing operational openings, the KGB oligarchy flexed its muscles, testing our young President. The Secretary of State and the President babbled about "re-setting" the relationship. Putin and his KGB minions surely reinvigorated covert operations. While they smiled at their "new best friends," a stable of covert reporters infiltrated the enemy.

Russia saw the strategic opening. Regaining her former glory as a super-power was in reach. Surely a message went out to all KGB stations: Our historic covert influence has borne fruit. Obama and his clique are our anti-American agents of change. Reach out. Intimidate. Influence. Negotiate. Accelerate developmentals. Lend a sympathetic ear. Help them destroy their own country.

Obama was nurtured in the fertile center of Soviet covert influence—Columbia University. KGB's file on Columbia dates back to one of the first Soviet illegals. Werner Rakov, a Soviet trade representative, enrolled in Columbia in 1925. Paul Massing, a "social researcher" spied for the KGB, and helped his wife, Heidi, recruit members of the forerunner of the CIA.

Whittaker Chambers studied at Columbia before joining the Communist Party of the USA (CPUSA). Elizabeth Bentley did too. Bill Ayers earned his Education degrees at Columbia Teachers College. Cy Oggins, a hapless American agent for the KGB, shot dead in the basement of the KGB's headquarters, studied at Columbia in 1920s. And young Barry Obama earned a degree there.

One of the Soviet's supreme covert influence agents, Dr. George S. Counts, joined the International Institute at Columbia Teachers College in 1927. With no background, he was hired to specialize in Russia. Immediately sent to Moscow, and provided with a highly intelligent Russian assistant, he was recruited by the KGB within a year. His powerful covert influence operations, guided by the Soviets, planted the seeds of anti-American political correctness that destroyed our education system. Even today American education students cite Counts in their radical dissertations.

The KGB is not all-powerful. They are very tenacious, focused, and professional. They never take their eye off the ball. Even when the Politburo was purging KGB officers—calling them home and putting a bullet in their neck, they still operated successfully, up to the day they got on the boat for Moscow. The agents they left behind were well-trained and continued operating. Their covert influence operations did not need KGB officers to maintain. Once they were begun, funded, and operating, the covert influence took on a life of its own. Like kudzu devouring Georgia, political correctness has engulfed our country.

The KGB targeted the three main cultural transmitters: education/academia, the media, and Hollywood. The anti-American messages (America is a racist, foreigner-hating, sexist imperialistic, hating culture), implanted like advertising, went viral. A KGB officer did not need to be at every meeting of radicals. They chose their influence agents carefully. They provided the American "Willing Accomplices" with the messages, and then got out of the way. The message exploded across American society.

The KGB influence agent at Columbia, Dr. Counts, created the anti-American point of view in education and academia. In his 1932 speeches "Dare the School Build a New Social Order," declared to American teachers that they needed to "change society." Counts told American teachers that they had a duty to bring about a new age of collectivism. Counts told teachers that the "age of individualism is dead."

The Russian spies today are only the tail end of Russia's fixation on the Great Enemy, America. The questions today are: Do our protectors believe in traditional America, or in destroying traditional America? Is this the change some of us believed in? Does change mean the final destruction of the America we once knew and loved?

Chapter 9
Pelaez, the Hispanic Press, and Russian Covert Influence

BigJournalism, July 9, 2010

The FBI arrested fiery New York columnist, Vicky Pelaez in late June. An editor and writer for the Spanish language newspaper El Diario La Prensa, she was charged with being an unregistered agent of the Russian government. Her far-left, anti-American columns won accolades from American Progressives, and from the Hispanic diaspora in the U.S. Released on bail to home detention during the Fourth of July long weekend, she now awaits further legal developments.

A sample from a Pelaez editorial in El Diario, translated from Spanish scorched the policies of her adopted country: "...refusing to hear ... the popular resistance and the opinion of the majority of countries in the world, the Big Boss [the United States] supported the putchists' ... illegal [Honduran] presidential elections..." Pelaez finished her anti-American rant, written in her comfortable suburban house in Yonkers, NY, with a tired revolutionary screech, "as long as injustice and poverty remain dominant, the struggle will continue." (El Diario, December 1, 2009)

Soviet intelligence operatives (the KGB), starting in the 1920s, recruited agents in the press to influence American opinion. The goal of the communist influence messages, as directed by Vladimir Lenin, was to destroy "the Main Enemy" from within. Lenin used this tactic, learned in his own Revolution, because he knew the Soviet army was too weak to take on the American military.

The influence message, boiled down to its essence was, and is, "America is an irredeemably racist, sexist, foreigner-hating, imperialistic, war-mongering country that deserves to be destroyed." Repeating this message over and over, like an advertising campaign, rooted the message deep in the psyches of the past several generations. The ultimate result of decades of propagating this message through the press, education and academia, and Hollywood has been the attitude known as Political Correctness (PC).

For nearly a century, Russian intelligence operations have exploited our openness, and the American commitment to individual rights. The Russians know that an American, regardless of origin or recent citizenship, is allowed to speak freely and criticize the government. To exploit our weaknesses, the KGB has honed their influence techniques. They prefer to use leftists, minorities, and women (Pelaez is a three-fer, combining all three desirable attributes) as their agents.

When confronted or challenged, these agents claim oppression. This was modeled during successful influence operations in the 1950s. The operations involved influencing reactions to the arrest, trial, and execution of the Soviet covert collection agents, Ethel and Julius Rosenberg. This was a textbook case study of Russian intelligence apparatchiks' response to exposure. The technique can be summarized as: "Admit nothing. Deny everything. Make counter-accusations."

The template of the Pelaez operation is familiar to experts in Russian covert influence operations. In the early 1920s, the KGB targeted a foreign-born journalist of dubious background, Walter Duranty. When he landed in Moscow, on assignment with the New York Times, he was immediately picked up by KGB officers. Their assessment of Duranty would have only taken a week or two. In that short period of "time on target," the KGB's smooth operators would have discovered Duranty's myriad vulnerabilities.

Arriving in Moscow Duranty would have been quickly assessed as an egotistical, one-legged opium addicted hack journalist who craved attention and sexual contact with girls of a certain age. In short order the KGB provided Duranty with a renovated apartment in the devastated Russian capital, a car and driver, a house-keeper-with-benefits, access to sources of wine, women and song, and numerous official Soviet sources, exclusively for Duranty.

KGB-facilitated sources provided Duranty with scoops on numerous stories. His house-keeper provided him with a live-in sexual outlet (his borderline insane wife left Moscow after a short period of residence). And the non-stop rounds of wine, women, and song stroked his ego. He was soon hailed as the dean of foreign correspondents in Moscow. He held court at hotels and bars frequented by Americans and westerners, always on the look-out for young girls he could impress with his power.

While the KGB fed Duranty stories, they met his other needs, for a time. The house-keeper gave birth to Duranty's only child. However, after Duranty helped arrange the US diplomatic recognition of the USSR, and covered up Stalin's forced famine in the Ukraine, the KGB cut loose its unstable agent of influence, and Duranty faded into oblivion.

Today we see the same pattern of influence operations against the American media. One of the most important demographic slices in America is the Hispanic population. With Spanish language media providing direct targeting, covert influence operators find targeting Hispanics quite easy.

Pelaez arrived in New York in 1988 and established herself as an expert on leftist issues. She burrowed deep into the Spanish language press. From journalist to commentator, she editorialized freely. She was widely quoted in Hispanic media, and frequently highlighted by Cuban propaganda vehicles.

If the allegations against Pelaez are accurate, Russian covert influence operations would seem to be following a well-worn path of tradecraft. Using tried and true recruiting techniques, the Russian operators methodically assess the motivations of their targets. Using the targets' unique motivations, the KGB recruits them as agents. They become Willing Accomplices in anti-American influence operations. Sometimes the agents are witting of their KGB control, sometimes they are not. From the FBI's reports, it appears that Pelaez was likely fully witting of her KGB sponsorship.

Pelaez, originally a citizen of Peru, infiltrated the US after a suspicious, one-day "kidnapping" by Peruvian communist rebels. Soon after, she was granted asylum to enter the US. Ironically, her asylum request was apparently based on the threat of retribution from the communists.

The use of a Russian-born immigrant, hiding in plain sight as a KGB controller is another bit of classic Russian tradecraft. A husband acting as controller for a wife is uncommon, but not unheard of (see again, the Rosenberg case). Pelaez's husband appears to have confessed to the FBI, admitting his birth in Russia and his work for the KGB. It's likely that his role was as a principal agent, acting as the go-between for his wife and their KGB handlers.

In extensive research into KGB covert influence operations, I have developed a three question sequence to identify suspected agents. Has the subject traveled to Russia, or been subject to communist assessment and development somewhere else? After exposure to assessment and development, does the subject's publicly expressed point of view match that of the Russian party line? After development by the KGB, did the subject's material circumstances change for the better?

A quick analysis of Pelaez's life reveals that the answers to all three questions match the profile of other Russian agents. She was "kidnapped" for one day by communist rebels. During that period of control by the communists, she obtained an exclusive interview with their leader. Since this incident, her point of view has matched the

KGB's anti-American point of view almost perfectly. Finally, with asylum in the US, a high-profile job in New York, and her husband's work as a college professor, Pelaez's material circumstances have definitely improved.

Most Americans are justifiably confused and skeptical about the FBI's charges against Pelaez and her alleged co-conspirators. But to those who study the Russians' historical influence operations, the revelations are another chapter in the KGB's continuing efforts to destroy American culture and society. These arrests should serve as a wake-up call to all Americans who treasure our unique qualities—rough and ready, rugged individualism, commitment to liberty, and belief in the free enterprise system.

Chapter 10
Covert Influence Target: American Education—Obama, Ayers, and Counts

Oct 2008

American academics and educators who carried on long-term relationships with Soviets or communism. They developed both overt and covert ties to the Soviet Union. An ex-communist, Louis Budenz provided a guide to understanding the backgrounds of academics who, following the communist conspiratorial methodology, refused to state their true beliefs or communist affiliation. Budenz revealed the actions and affiliations of academics from the 1930s to the 1960s, when it was impossible to be an overt Marxist in the US. KGB-sponsored fronts provided academia with cover for their actions in support of the Soviets. One Columbia University professor, Bernhard Stern, was a member of 40 communist fronts during the immediate post WWII years. At the same time, Stern testified before Congress and pled the 5th Amendment, refusing to answer questions on the grounds that he might incriminate himself.

The 5th Amendment ploy was regularly used by the communists when faced with exposure. While pleading the 5th is not an automatic indictment, and is a Constitutional right, we can now look back at the historical record and see that virtually every one of the witnesses before the House Un-American Activities Committee who pled the 5th were communists. As Budenz, the ex-communist, pointed out, you cannot identify communists by their words, but rather by their actions. If it walks like a duck, it is very likely a duck. Stern is but one example of the academics who were at the beck and call of the Soviets, using KGB tactics to spread the noxious anti-American covert influence payloads. And their use of the covert action motto—admitting nothing, denying everything, and making counter-accusations is another confirmation of their covert action links.

In writing my book, *Willing Accomplices* I examined the KGB infiltration of the American Kindergarten to 12th grade (K-12) education system in the early 1900s through the 1960s. The Soviets did not neglect their covert efforts to infect the roots of American society. As Budenz said, "In undermining a nation such as the United States, the infiltration of the educational process is of prime importance...The Communists have accordingly made the invasion of schools...the major consideration in their psychological warfare designed to control the American mind." (Budenz, p. 208) In 1937, during the height of the Popular Front surge of support for socialism, American communist teachers were exhorted by an article in a Communist magazine to "...affect the children's thinking, and they must mobilize other teachers...without exposing themselves." (Budenz, p. 209) The American education mafia was diving deeply into John Dewey's philosophy of Pragmatism, which holds that there is no real truth, and no absolute good or evil. This theory fed into the hands of the Communist covert influence operators.

Because the leaders of the Progressive educationists wrote a lot, we have a good record of the communist inspired philosophies that the transmitted into American classrooms. For example, George Counts was a carrier of the communist covert influence message into K-12 education. In the late 1920s, through the early 1930s, Counts traveled extensively in the USSR, where he was surely met and cultivated by the KGB. His book, Dare the Schools Build a New Social Order? (1932), reveals the goals of the Soviets in the title, annihilation of the American social order. Counts' covert influence operations were substantial. Russia provided him with a Soviet textbook, initially used in the Soviet Union as an indoctrination tool for children in their education system. The Russians provided Counts with an English translation, which he brought to America and published. His introduction to the book, New Russia's Primer: The Story of the Five-Year Plan (1931), waxed eloquently and enthusiastically in support of a collectivized economy. This book is a good example of a typical communist covert influence payload. Without actually calling for the communization of American society, and speaking in the coded language of covert influence, Counts laid the foundation of a logical and reasonable argument. Readers were left to come to their own conclusion that communism was the only path possible. In reality, even as Counts was writing his introduction, Stalin was carrying out unbelievably grotesque repression of the Russian masses. Counts' other writings similarly carried the communist covert influence message into American schools of education and elementary and high school classrooms.

John T. Flynn served on the Board of higher education for New York state from 1933 to 1944. During his tenure on the board of education, New York State undertook an investigation of communist infiltration of the education system. Flynn, a self defined liberal, could not believe the charges against numerous teachers, most of whom he knew personally. The trials conducted by the state resulted in guilty verdicts for a total of 35 teachers. According to Flynn, these teachers were not merely Socialists or leftists, but Communists. Flynn was shocked to discover the infiltration of his own system by the Communists. Clearly, the Communists were using the covert influence template of the KGB. Flynn spelled out very clearly what he saw the communist mission to be: "a seductive form of propaganda for collectivism – this propaganda takes the form of teaching openly as possible, cautiously if necessary three things. First, that our American system of private enterprise is a failure. Second, that our republic of limited powers is a mistake. Third, that our way of life must give way to a collectivist society in which the central State will own and operate, or plan and finance and control, the economic system." (Flynn, in Scott and Hill, p. 159)) Clearly Flynn, an educational bureaucrat, saw the results of the Communist covert influence operations. However, unable to see the forest for the trees, he focused on the 35 teachers who were found to be spreading the communist propaganda in his state schools, and was unaware of the great covert war unfolding around him.

Flynn, on the front lines of the struggle against the collectivization of American society, saw the enemy. He quotes from Counts' 17 volume study of social science in American schools, "... 'the age of individualism is closing and a new age of collectivism is emerging.' The report then proposed that the teachers go to work upon the minds of their pupils to prepare them for the new collectivist society."

Part Two

Intelligence Obliteration

Chapter 11
The Failed Puppet-master: Fire John Brennan

Originally published: Big Peace, February 2011

Late Thursday morning, President Obama's CIA Director, Leon Panetta (a former Congressman and White House Chief of Staff with zero intelligence community experience) testified to the House Intelligence Committee that Egyptian President Mubarak "will step down this evening."

Four hours later, Mubarak publicly announces that he is not stepping down, and that he rejected "any and all dictations from abroad," in a direct slap-down of Obama and his minions.

At the same hearing with Panetta, the Director of National Intelligence (DNI), James Clapper opined that the Egyptian-based Islamic extremist group, the Muslim Brotherhood (MB), was "largely secular."

Five days previously, Obama's hand-picked envoy to Egypt, Frank Wisner, after visiting the country, said that Mubarak must remain in power to manage the transition. Obama immediately retracted that statement, and Wisner disappeared.

Unfortunately, we would be lucky if it were only Panetta, Clapper, and Wisner mucking around. The big story is the Obama lackey we have not seen since the Maghreb Mutinies began, Obama's Czar for Terrorism, and de facto intelligence chief, John Brennan.

Brennan has sought out TV cameras at every opportunity since January 2009. He popped up to talk about any issue dealing with intelligence, terrorism, Arabs, or Islam. He took it upon himself to declare the words "war on terrorism, jihad, global war" off limits. He trumpeted his "summer in Indonesia," (like the President!), his semester abroad in Cairo, and his CIA station chief experience in "the region."

Burrowing into his lair on Pennsylvania Avenue, Brennan gathered the strings of the national intelligence infrastructure and became the intel bureaucracy puppet master. Hapless generals passed through the DNI position, each undermined by Brennan, perched next to his idol's throne, whispering in Obama's ear. Remember DNI Clapper telling Diane Sawyer he didn't know about "London." Who quickly chimed in with the proper answer? Why, it was Brennan—showing up the titular head of American intelligence.

To understand the Brennan shadow play going on behind the scenes in Egypt, you first must understand the man— he is a CIA analyst. To understand the man, you must understand the culture of the bureaucracy that he ascended from—the CIA's Directorate of Intelligence (DI), the nation's intelligence analysis belly button—and the type of person that culture produces.

A CIA analyst's life is like being in grad school, forever. Just like an academic, the analyst is evaluated on his record of "publications." Just like an academic, the analyst spends his time researching, writing, defending his work to committees, and trying to get his writing published. The big difference is that a CIA analyst has more resources, classified intelligence reports from operators around the world that an academic does not have. Otherwise, a CIA is a virtual clone of an academic.

Just as in academia, the point of the exercise (creating finished intelligence to guide U.S. policy makers) becomes lost in academic politics, backstabbing, ass kissing, and internecine scheming. Just as in academia, CIA analysts who want to move up yearn for a position closer to the se of bureaucratic power.

An analyst's most treasured professional accomplishment is to have a hand in the Presidential Daily Brief (PDB). An article published in the PDB can be the crowning achievement of an analyst's career. Circling the flame of power, like calculating moths, they try to get closer. The ultimate career position for a CIA analyst is to be the President's Briefer, the guy who carries the PDB in to the President every morning. If an analyst is allowed to do that only once in his lifetime, he can die happy, fulfilled. He's been to the mountaintop.

The other point that you must understand about analysts is what they are not. CIA analysts, regardless of what you've read or seen in Tom Clancy movies, are not spies. They do not manage spies. They do not recruit spies. They do not handle spies. They are not covert operators. They do not uncover secrets. They do not fast-rope from Blackhawks.

They sit in cubicles and research and write. Then they argue among themselves about what each other has written. Then they brief others on their articles. Then they do that again. And again, and again, and again. Because of the dreary reality of their lives, the analysts are allowed large budgets for travel. They travel to the countries in their portfolio, on boondoggle familiarization trips—which are more like vacations.

Many CIA analysts join the Agency believing the Tom Clancy hype. Once they learn what their job is, they can become bitter. And they can succumb to envy—of the operators who do recruit spies, travel the world under cover, meet and befriend exotic people, and plan and execute clandestine operations. There is a definite culture of envy in the CIA's DI.

Because of this envy, occasionally, when the CIA goes through one of its bouts of self-destructiveness, the director of the CIA appoints an analyst, to be the chief of an overseas operational station. And when a presidential administration is extremely anti-CIA, like the Clintons, it appoints an analyst to be in charge of the entire Directorate of Operations.

John Brennan is a CIA analyst. In his mind, he is the Tom Clancy hero—the analyst fast-roping into a crisis, sub-machine gun locked and loaded, ready to respond. But in reality, he is an academic with sharply honed in-fighting claws, ready to rip to shreds a rival's analytical piece so that his will be published.

Brennan clawed his way to the top of the analytical pile—he was President Clinton's PDB briefer. During the Bush presidency, he burrowed into the CIA bureaucracy, snuggling up to Clinton appointee DCI Tenet. He finished his career by standing up the failure-prone Terrorist Threat Integration Center (TTIC) and the National Counter-terrorism Center (NCTC), both of which were supposed to "connect the dots," which analysts failed to connect before the 9/11 attacks.

Brennan retired from NCTC and joined an intelligence contractor. NCTC then awarded his firm a contract to provide connect-the-dots analytical software. In the Christmas Day "panties-bomber" failed terrorist attack, NCTC, using Brennan's software, failed to connect the dots. Obama assigned Brennan to investigate the failure. Sweet work, if you can get it.

Now he's used those nasty analytical academic skills to worm his way into the clueless White House's foreign policy and intelligence inner sanctum. He hitched his wagon to Obama's star early, and has ridden it far. Nestled into his office in the White House, an analyst's nirvana, he has jealously built his intelligence empire. He is the de facto DNI, DCIA, and director of covert operations. Like a corrupt Turkish eunuch, manipulating a callow crown prince, he whispers in his ruler's ear and rivals disappear.

This background brings us up to today. The morning after Mubarak told Obama to leave Egypt alone, after the DNI said the MB is sort of like Knights of Columbus, after the DCIA said he's watching CNN and it looks like Mubarak will resign.

Where is John Brennan? Since the uprising began in Tunisia, until today, John Brennan has not appeared on national TV once. Now that you know his background, it should be easy to guess, as I'm doing. I don't have any inside knowledge, but I'd bet that our hero Brennan is ensconced in a five-star suite in Cairo, running what he believes is a cunning covert influence operation. My guess is that Mubarak's rejection of "dictations from abroad" should have been "dictations from John Brennan."

This massive cluster-failure of a foreign policy looks like an amateur operation, run by a wannabe operator. The one personality in the Obama administration that fits that description is John Brennan.

Egypt today is no place for a "semester abroad expert" political analyst to be allowed free rein. Obama, fire John Brennan today. Let the DNI that you and your party craved do his work. You have a huge intelligence collection and analysis infrastructure idling while Brennan plays his egomaniacal games.

Do the right thing. Bring Brennan back out of the shadows and put him to pasture. Let professionals do the job.

Chapter 12

Selective Progressive Outrage? Extra-judicial Killings or Water-boarding, Take Your Pick

Originally published: BigPeace, December 9, 2010

Newsweek first revealed that the Bush administration used harsh interrogation tactics to obtain intelligence from terrorist masterminds in 2004. American Progressives leapt at the chance to attack the evil, war-mongering, Halliburton-loving, Cheney-controlled Bush. Their pious, humanitarian tinged caterwauling was heard non-stop, coast to coast, on every Progressive media outlet, from every college campus, and from Hollywood.

Progressive hand-wringing over the horror of water-boarding grew to epic proportions. They called for war crimes tribunals for the unrepentant fascist scum working to keep them safe from Al Qaeda. Hazing of prisoners at Abu Ghraib—in which helpless prisoners were stripped naked and forced to wear demeaning clothing—became, in the fevered Progressive imagination, tantamount to Auschwitz.

When I attended the International Ethics in Intelligence conference in 2006, the Progressive academics in attendance were mainly interested in discussing one topic—torture. Of the hundreds in attendance, I only ran across two other members who had ever been intelligence officers in the field. Few of the presenters on Torture, or the myriad related "ethical" issues had ever been at the pointy end of the spear. They lectured on "Just War Theory" and Hegelian ethics as applied to an Aristotelian world view, or other pseudo-intellectual rot. To a person, they condemned the Bush administration's use of harsh interrogation tactics. The Guantanamo Bay prison camp was another popular target of revulsion.

Fast forward just four years later. Torture is out of the news. Gitmo remains open. The media quietly reports that CIA "drone strikes" (missile attacks from an unmanned aerial vehicles) and associated "targeted killings" have sky-rocketed since Obama gained control of the covert action elements of the U.S. Government.

Our new President, the Progressive hero, rules the Executive Branch. The Executive controls the CIA, and all law enforcement and intelligence, including covert action. Covert killings, including UAV targeted killings, require a "finding" to be signed by the President.

In 2006 there were a reported total of two drone attacks in Pakistan, which killed a reported 23 people. In the first 11 months of 2010 the Obama administration is reportedly carried out 106 attacks in Pakistan, with a death toll of up to 857. Evidently, Obama's left hand has been quite busy signing findings between rounds of golf and elbow-banging sessions on the hardwood court.

The faux outrage over water-boarding was over the top. Progressives vowed revenge on the Bush administration members who had reviewed and approved the harsh methods. The Progressive reaction to low-level, untrained jailers playing pranks on defenseless prisoners at Abu Ghraib created world-wide ill-will against the U.S. and our interests. In response, Americans were taken hostage and brutally tortured. Terrorists sawed and hacked the heads off of American and other allied hostages. They shared their gory work online.

The Progressive outrage machine seems to have run out of steam. Where is the outrage over the extra-judicial killings of 857 people, in Pakistan alone? We are not at war with Pakistan. The Obama administration waffles on whether we are still at war or not, and if so, with whom. People, including American and allied citizens, are alleged to be members of terrorist organizations. They are alleged to be planning terrorist attacks.

The Obama administration made a public vow to use legal and defensible approaches to combating "man-caused contingencies," or whatever their political commissars have decided to call terrorism. They vowed to close Gitmo. They vowed to bring clarity to dealing with the poor innocents the bad Bushies had snatched from their cradles and sent to the prison on Cuba.

Their vain, self-congratulatory certainty of moral superiority was, and is, a sham. Now that Obama and his minions control the covert action apparatus, it has shifted into high gear. They operate in ways that were not even conceivable during the Bush administration. American, international, and local laws be damned.

While we surely need to have counter-terrorist operations, we also need to consider American and international law when we take those actions. A German legislator, a member of the Left party (leftovers from East Germany), pointed out that "Obama is not God," after a German was killed. Maybe the understatement of the century, but I believe that unrepentant communist is quite prescient. It is possible that Obama's extra-judicial killings could be his Watergate. Who knew what and when?

Anwar al-Awlaki is certainly affiliated with terrorism. He clearly inspires al Qaeda wannabes, including the Ft Hood terrorist, Nidal Hassan, and the hapless Christmas 2009 Panties Bomber.

It appears that Obama's policy is to target for extra-judicial killing by a UAV missile American citizens who inspire terrorists to plan attacks. Considering the actual, armed attack on the Discovery Channel by eco-terrorist ("humans are filth") James Lee, Al Gore should probably check in with the White House regularly.

Chapter 13
Iran, Mexico, Furious Assassins: Manufactured crisis, World War III?

October 2011

As I predicted the day after his election, Obama and his radical clique are hell-bent on destroying the traditional USA. Stymied in their overt attempts—ObamaCare, trillion-dollar stimulus deficit spending, financial reforms, etc.—resorted to covert actions. This is their comfort zone—lie, obfuscate, cover-up, excuse, deny, make counter-accusations.

PC-Progressives are liars by profession. They cannot reveal their true beliefs. If they did, they would be run out of the country on a rail. So they lie, obfuscate, conceal. Thus, PC-Progressives take very well to official covert actions

Covert action requires lying. But the lying is officially sanctioned. The Obama administration, the most radical anti-American administration in history is immersed now in official lying—covert actions in Yemen, Pakistan, Egypt, Libya, Mexico. What will the end game be? God help us.

Eric Holder, no stranger to counter-constitutional measures is being slowly encircled by constitutional investigations. The subpoena he dreaded arrived in his office this week.

Anticipating the Fast and Furious subpoena, walls closing in around him, Holder-Obama sprung a surprise.

A manufactured crisis leading to war is the only way out for these malefactors. Like their role model, FDR, they believe that the only way for their Keynesian economics to heal the country is to destroy it. The only atonement for

America's imagined past sins is to wash them away in blood—oceans of blood. As their castles in the air dissolve, both domestically and internationally, the only possible PC-Progressive response is to start a war—the bigger, the better.

Just like their ideological fathers, Lenin and Stalin, the Obama-Holder-Hillary clique must instigate international turmoil.

What better way to instigate turmoil than an FBI-DEA entrapment operation? Convince a poor schmuck Iranian with ties to the Ayatollah's regime that he's dealing with big-wig narcos. Talk him into a big operation—"let's whack the Saudi ambassador! That's the ticket!" Get him talking about the operation on tape. Then, when needed, publicize the bust, fan the flames of hysteria.

Presto! Change-o! Headlines about corruption, cronyism, perjury, selling firearms to Mexican drug dealers, loner Obama, loser Holder, Hillary biding her time, Republicans surging, whacko-PC-Progressives drumming and defecating on Wall Street—all fade away.

Manufacture a crisis. Publicize it. Fan the flames. Beat the drums for war. Who can resist? Conservative war-hawks are drawn in. The PC-Progressives, now that they command the military, are all for it.

Ever hear of the Tonkin Gulf incident?

The more things change. Gird your loins—this will not be clean, or pretty.

Chapter 14
Political Correctness Killed 7 at Khost

Originally appeared: FrontPageMag, April 29, 2010

Last December 30th, a horrific bombing snuffed out the lives of seven American patriots. We can only wish that the same blast had snuffed out the Politically Correct policies that led to those young peoples' deaths. With heavy hearts, and a salute to our fallen heroes, it is fitting and proper that we should soberly consider the bureaucracy that placed those brave but inexperienced officers at a forward firebase in a war zone.

Political correctness killed the CIA operations officer, the analyst, and the others supporting the meeting, just as surely as the blast and fragments from the package strapped under the bomber's robe did. Every clandestine meeting with a terrorist is dangerous and potentially deadly. The meeting itself is a tiny part of the operation. Training and preparation, planning and cultural knowledge, understanding your asset's personality, motivations, needs, and problems, are just a few of the issues that an operations officer must juggle and attempt to control. But the first step is the selection process itself that chooses candidates who will become operations officers in a war zone.

When the meeting is held in conjunction with a foreign intelligence service, as the presence of the Jordanian intelligence officer seems to suggest this one was, another layer of complications are introduced into an already complicated situation. Language, control, compatible goals, strategy, tactics, all must be coordinated, discussed, hashed out, and agreed upon with the partner. Vastly separated by culture and objectives, a CIA ops officer and her foreign counterpart must dance down a delicately balanced tightrope.

By their very nature, penetrations of terrorist organizations are dangerous, crafty, deceptive, and hard to handle. Whether the source is playing the role of a terrorist at the behest of a hostile intelligence handler, or is a real terrorist cooperating with friendly intelligence officers, the key element of the source's personality is deception.

A terrorist is not usually the most savory character. In fact, he probably has a long history of walking on the wrong side of the law. Arrests, jail, detention, prison, living double lives, lying about his true intentions, beliefs and plans are second nature to a terrorist. Crimes, deceit, double-dealing, conspiracy, murder, rape and robbery are every day facts of life for a terrorist. He has been involved in black market schemes, counterfeiting, visa fraud, online fraud, identity theft, and multiple other schemes, cons, and rackets.

As if the background of the target does not pose enough challenges, remember that the target comes from a culture so different from that of middle America that, for the average American, the terrorist source may as well be from Pluto.

The target is likely a Middle Eastern male, probably native Arabic-speaking. He is also a member of a vastly complex, inter-woven network of social, tribal, national, religious, clan, ethnic, and other groups. The flavor of Arabic he speaks, and the name he bears immediately identify him of a certain clan/tribe/ethnicity. He practices, or used to practice, a form of Islam that is strongly affected by his tribal and ethnic background.

He likely has participated in some sort of Islamic revival movement. He has probably traveled abroad, perhaps to the West. He has been bombarded with Western culture from the day he was born. He has a grasp of English, at least in reading. He probably has been educated in a technical discipline. He is of above average intelligence. He is able to use charm, and knows how to manipulate Americans. He has a strong, though misguided, understanding of American culture and lifestyles. His view of Americans is not complex. He knows that American men are big, play football and drink a lot of beer. He knows American women are blonde, have large breasts and are eager to engage in casual sex with strangers they have just met. He admires, covets, and loathes the American lifestyle, economy and culture. He is interested in converting any American he meets to Islam.

He is smooth like a snake, and would rather slip a knife into your American ribs than deal with you. He is meeting with an American intelligence officer for his own reasons, which very likely have nothing to do with the reasons the American is meeting with him.

While every case is different, that is a rough profile of a potential terrorist asset. It might also be helpful to review who a terrorist asset is not. This man is not a diplomat. He does not attend embassy cocktail parties. He is not a European sophisticate looking for an American contact to discuss the Copenhagen round of Global Warming talks. The terrorist is not impressed with American ideas of equality or Political Correctness. He does not fear a sexual harassment lawsuit. He shares not one of PC America's concerns about "offensive speech," or "the glass ceiling." He is not interested in hearing the American view of the Middle East.

A CIA ops officer has the task of meeting, assessing, developing a close friendship with, and then recruiting the terrorist described above. The most highly coveted recruitment would be a member of an enemy terrorist organization. If that terrorist had, or could nurture a connection to, or information about the whereabouts of Osama bin Laden, the recruitment would be a ticket to superstardom for the ops officer.

Who are the CIA ops officers that are pitted against this hardest of hard targets? What is the profile that the CIA uses to find and hire the operators to work against international slimeballs? Based on the CIA's profile for hiring, you would think this job requires the same skills as an investment banker, an NGO advisor, an accountant, a lawyer, or another high-class professional.

CIA's recruitment center, flooded with applicants after 9/11, set an arbitrary minimum undergraduate GPA of 3.75 for a candidate to be considered. Falling back on traditional profiles of clandestine service candidates, created during the Cold War, the CIA filled huge classes with eager young faces. The typical recruit came from a prestige school, with a BA or MA in International Relations, Political Science, Area Studies, or other soft liberal arts. The recruit had studied a foreign language, to less than fluent proficiency. Since a class-action lawsuit in 1993, it is now more likely that the recruit is female.

She had foreign experience, probably a semester, or a year, in an American university's study abroad program, most likely in Europe. She was in her mid-20s. She had never been arrested, never been involved in anything shady or illegal, never used drugs, and drank alcohol moderately. She sweated through her polygraph test, probably the first time she has ever been questioned by a hostile authority.

After passing the academic screening and an interview, candidates passed a security clearance, including a thorough background check, drug testing, psychological screening ("I'm fascinated by fire: T or F"), and a polygraph exam. Those with arrest and criminal records are deemed unsuitable. A rowdy, street-smart male is likely to be screened out at some point in the process.

These recruits are the type of kids you would want your child bringing home as a life partner. They come from all the best schools, eager, arrogant, confident, swaggering, innocent, and full of potential. But are they the right candidates for dealing with cunning terrorists?

The answer should be clear. Absolutely not. The recruits make very good choir boys and girls, squeaky clean, innocent, naïve, and wholly unsuited to deal with terrorists. However, the problems with the CIA's process just begin at recruitment. You think that these fresh kids will be trained. Training could be used to create some of the street-smarts required to deal with terrorists and other scumbag sources. But the training to prepare the choir boys to deal with slimeballs would take years and years. They only have a few months. .

Mandatory sexual harassment training in the CIA is rigorous and repeated. More like communist "self-criticism" sessions, this training infuriates most males, and empowers most females. The video vignettes used in the training paint with a broad brush. Males are pig-headed imbecilic, racist predators. Females are hard-working, put-upon, victims of the white male hierarchy. Past lack of female representation in management has given way to a flood of newly minted Senior Intelligence Service females, and mid-level female managers up and down the chain of command, including in the field.

The "street smarts" training that CIA operations officers go through is quite helpful, if the recruit brings a high level of street sense to the first day of class. If not, the training is all but wasted on the naïve innocents. If you've never been worried about being detected by the police, if you've never been arrested, if you've never lied about your activities, if you've never cased a location to prepare for an illegal activity, if you've never sweet-talked someone into (or out of) something, the training is a confusing whirlwind of alien concepts.

The recruits, selected for their high GPAs, and pristine backgrounds, gamely go through the motions. They learn the basics, and the concepts, intellectually, but for the vast majority, they are in a frightening upside-down universe of moral ambiguity and repulsive manipulation. Where right is wrong, and wrong is right; where you must become best friends with your worst enemy; this is the universe of deadly con-games.

While it is true that females are much better, generally speaking, at manipulating, and reading subtle signs in, others the unspoken issue of sex and sexual expectations greatly complicates a female ops officer's attempts to ply her craft. Political correctness dictates that the CIA and its experienced ops officers should not mention this fact of nature, and in fact, they pretend it does not exist. Unlike other, highly effective intel services, which use sex as part of their arsenal, the PC CIA treats every ops officer as if they are interchangeable.

After training, the newly minted female ops officer is assigned to a post in "the Sand Box," Afghanistan or Iraq, or to more genteel post. In neither one does she learn anything about the realities of the street culture of her targets. What she does learn, and become acculturated to, are the realities of American government culture. She learns how to survive and prosper in the bureaucracy. At either the fire base, or genteel circles, she becomes adept at negotiating the social maze of American PC culture. And while this is important for her career, it does not advance America's fight against terrorists.

In human intel ops, initial attempts at making contact with a potential source might involve an arranged meeting in a public place, or the source may walk-in to volunteer. When a female ops officer approaches a stranger in public, especially an Arab male, the sexual electricity is super-charged. Even with a walk-in, the ops officer is thrust into a highly emotionally charged relationship, with an immediate need to begin to sort out truth from lies and distortions.

Even if operating in the same culture and language, such situations are extremely difficult to handle. But when attempts at befriending and manipulating take place in an alien culture and language, maybe through an interpreter, the relationship is so complicated as to be unmanageable. A male ops officer has a difficult enough time in navigating through the twists and turns of a development, without sexual baggage hanging over each meeting.

PC denial of reality may not have much immediate effect in other US government offices, like the Department of Agriculture, but in CIA operations, the effects are immediate and obvious, to an objective observer. Painful as it may be for the PC crowd to admit, we must adapt to the target culture. We cannot force our targets to adapt to our culture. We should not send a woman in to do a job, and pretend she is not handicapped by her sex.

The father of one of the dead officers knew instinctively that a war zone was not the right place for a girl who had graduated from Keith Country Day School and Colby College, which offers a semester abroad program in Spain, and one in France. The bereaved father recalled: "I begged her not to go, I said, 'Do you know how dangerous that is? That's for soldiers.'"

Acknowledging this reality does not demean the work of old, new, or current female ops officers. They are doing their best, and are patriots, one and all. Any exception that one may cite (as there are highly effective female ops officers), simply proves the rule. They clearly have a role to play in the CT intel war. However, just as in our armed forces, where women are not allowed in combat roles, we should use the debacle at Khost as impetus to sift PC dreams of equality from the realities of operating against terrorists.

Chapter 15
Solving CIA's PC Problems—Counter-terrorism Corps of Collectors

Originally appeared in Front Page Mag; June 2, 2010

In an earlier article ("PC Casualties") I examined the dire effects of more than a decade of Political Correctness (PC) at the CIA. The most visible effect was the tragic death of seven CIA employees during a covert meeting on a forward operating base in Afghanistan.

The focus of the CIA is no longer on conducting effective intelligence operations against America's enemies. Their focus is now, like most US government entities, bureaucratic survival, and establishing a "diverse" workforce. Their affirmative action approach to selecting and promoting operations officers resulted in seven dead at Khost.

However, there are many more insidious effects that are unseen to the general public. Those who care about the safety and security of our country, and the viability of our civilian national covert action and intelligence collection organization, must speak out against the destructive effects of PC in the CIA, and its debilitating effects on covert operations.

Speaking out is not enough. As a successful counter-terrorism (CT) intelligence operative, a successful recruiter, and a successful instructional designer, I am compelled to share suggestions for change and improvement in our civilian CT and covert action efforts. My suggestions are based on a unique combination of experiences, education and training, which may provide valuable insights into future selection and training of operatives. The current, broken bureaucracy will be replaced with a specialized Counter-terrorism Corps of Collectors (CCC).

First, the CCC must conduct a needs assessment. What are the desired outcomes? What are the working conditions?

What are the skills/experience/education/background required for candidates to be successful American CT operators?

Head-to-head, toe-to-toe, sitting cross-legged on a rug on the sand, under a tent in the desert, camels hobbled nearby, sweet mint tea flowing, leaning on a cushion, fingering prayer beads, Mohammed Atta and his brethren only want to kill you. They are only concerned about the quickest, most efficient, most deadly terrorist action to bring down "the Great Satan." This requires cross-cultural skills in our target cultures.

The job of a counter-terrorism operations officer is to recruit penetrations of these terrorists. To get to know the Islamic extremists. To get inside their heads, understand their innermost desires, needs, motivations, thoughts, and feelings. And then to manipulate those motivations.

Terrorists are criminals. They break the law every day—immigration fraud, credit card fraud, robbery, and other crimes. Lying, cheating and stealing are as natural to them as breathing. Hiding among your victims requires you to live a lie, at least until the moment that you act. But up until that moment, a terrorist is like a thief in the dark—every action and deed criminal and furtive. Manipulating terrorists requires a deep understanding of the criminal mindset.

The working conditions in CCC operations are likely to be primitive and nomad-like. Whether working in the field with foreigners who share the culture of our targets, or working in a war zone, regardless, the conditions are not up to American comfort standards. Living rough requires experience in primitive conditions.

The requirements for this job can be summarized as in two areas, physical and mental. Mentally: to think like a criminal, to get in the mind of an Islamic extremist, to understand what motivates a determined homicidal terrorist, the ability to manipulate people for operational purposes. Physically: the skills to live in harsh environments.

With the conditions and required skills and experience identified, all that is left in our needs analysis is to identify a list of education/experiences that might lead a candidate's possession of the required background. In the analysis of this list of required traits, we ignore those things not required—including all the protected classes of traits—gender, religion, race, disability. The only thing that matters in this most important of jobs is ability to get the job done—countering terrorists.

To develop the mindset of a criminal, one is most likely to have been involved in some type of criminal activity. A candidate very likely can only truly understand the way of thinking of criminals by taking part in some kind of criminal activity. A short-hand way of describing this skill-set is "street smarts." Someone who knows what it's like to be both predator and prey, on the street. This requires intelligence, and experience on the streets. Valuable experience includes being a victim of a crime, as well as thinking like a criminal.

To develop an understanding of Islamic extremists, a candidate needs to have lived among them, day to day, eating with them, and sharing their dreams and disappointments. Either living among, with, or as one of them, a candidate should have had prior experience with Islamic extremists.

To manipulate and motivate our terrorist targets, a candidate must have experience in sales, teaching, training, coaching, or other related fields. Street-savvy cunning is more applicable than a BA in communications.

Experience living in harsh environments could come from the military, scouting, or other high adventure activities. Using this package of skills for American CT operations requires, maybe above all else, a love of the greatest country in the world.

We now have a good picture of our ideal candidate. He (or she) will have: spent time on the wrong side of the law; a well-developed street sense; a deep, cross-cultural understanding of Islamic extremists; experience in manipulating others for ulterior motives; ability to survive in harsh environments, and a desire to apply these skills to counter-terrorism operations for the protection and survival of the USA.

With this needs assessment-based candidate profile, we can now begin the search for CCC candidates. The CCC profile is 180 degrees opposite from the current profile used to recruit ops officers at the CIA. The current requirements include: minimum of a bachelors degree with a superior GPA; the ability to write clearly and accurately; ability to work independently and as part of a team; and "international experience." This can include semesters abroad in Paris, Rome, or London. The profile is an academic with some international interest or experience.

But our analysis of the skill-set required for the CCC shows that academic expertise has nothing to do with the actual work. Street smarts are far more important than academics. Cross-cultural experiences are more important than a high GPA.

The CCC candidate profile looks like the requirements for the operatives in the old movie, "The Dirty Dozen." They were recruited from a military prison. We do not necessarily have to go to prisons, but we do need to open up the recruiting process. We cannot just send retired secretaries to college job fairs.

After recruiting CCC candidates, we are faced with a dilemma. These candidates are so far out of the mainstream of the CIA that they are fundamentally different. We need to realize this, and from the outset, create a separate environment for them. As the Army's Special Forces train and deploy separate, but parallel to, the regular Army, so should the CCC be separate from the mainstream CIA. It may eventually supplant the mainstream CIA altogether, but in the beginning, it should stand separate, in recruitment, training, and deployment.

Our street-smart CCC trainees will take quickly to the tradecraft training. Since they are not required to write their own reports, however, the CCC training will include extensive exercises of providing oral reports to trained reports officers.

For terrorism ops, writing and academic knowledge pale in importance compared to street smarts. Written communication about operations will be done by trained reports officers, working with our CCC officers. Working as a team with the CCC ops officers, these traditional academically-oriented officers can craft beautiful ops cables after debriefing our CCC officers.

The CCC operators, like the movie's Dirty Dozen, will require close and constant supervision. Like Telly Savalas, managers will need to stay close to our CCC officers. The managers must understand the special needs of the CCC. This could be a very difficult job, much like managing a wild heavy-weight boxer. The CIA is already top-heavy with middle-managers. With a little training they should be able to handle the new counter-terror cadre.

This program is not to denigrate the need for other types of collectors. The traditional collector—genteel, caught up in the capital city whirl of social engagements, cocktail parties and 5-star restaurants will probably always be needed. But for the war we are fighting now, the CIA must renew itself, and create a specialized Counter-terrorism Corps of Collectors.

Chapter 16

Insane Counter-terror Bureaucracy Endangers Americans

January 2010

This past Christmas Day, Obama's Keystone Kops responded to a "man-made crisis" in Detroit. The resulting confusion and chaos laid bare their utter incompetence and the failure of their strategy to deal with terrorist attacks against America.

While the counter-terror big-wigs were skiing, street cops from the FBI took on a task for which they were totally unprepared. And that is the real crime in the Obama/Holder/Brennan counter-terrorism strategy.

The truth is that America is less safe because the Obama administration relies on law enforcement tactics in the on-going Global War on Terror. The Director of National Intelligence (DNI) who had been missing from the national conversation about the PantiesBomber in Detroit, surfaced and let slip a glimpse of the truth in testimony before Congress two weeks ago.

Dennis Blair said that the Nigerian terrorist should have been handled as an enemy combatant, and interrogated by the Obama/Holder special interrogation unit. This unit was announced months ago as Obama's "smart" solution to what Obama and Holder called "torture" in previous terrorist interrogations. Then, Robert Mueller, the head of the FBI, surfaced the next day and said that the FBI-led interrogation team does not even exist yet!

Like many smart guys, Obama confuses his eloquent speeches with on-the-ground results. However, in this case, let's look at the "brilliant strategy" a bit more closely. Maybe Obama's failure to implement it could be seen as a blessing in disguise.

The FBI is the world's best at investigating crimes on its turf, and walking the case through the US's prosecution system. The FBI is also very good at enticing potential bad guys in America into illegal schemes, like blowing up the Sears Tower. They are also very good at publicizing their successes, following J. Edgar Hoover's excellent public relations campaigns.

There are two important issues to understand when considering the FBI's successes. The first is the location of the FBI's turf. The FBI's turf is America. The second is one word—prosecution. FBI agents are rewarded and promoted based on their arrest, prosecution and conviction records. FBI agents in America sit on the top tier of the law enforcement community. On their turf, they have near total freedom to operate.

A gross simplification of their method of operating—an agent walks into an office in Raleigh. He flashes his badge, lets his coat slip open, allowing the office manager a glimpse of the agent's holstered semi-automatic handgun. The agent says, "I'm Special Agent Jim Smith, FBI." Agent Smith is immediately provided full access to whatever, or whoever, he wants.

In direct opposition to this "badge and gun" law enforcement culture is the CIA. The CIA's operations officers are among the world's best at gathering and reporting intelligence in foreign countries. The CIA is also the world's best at leveraging relationships with foreign intelligence, and foreign security services. The CIA has targeted and collected against foreign terrorist organizations, around the globe, for decades, on foreign soil.

CIA's competencies are encapsulated best by one word— foreign. The CIA's mission is foreign intelligence. CIA operations officers are rewarded and promoted based on their abilities to recruit foreign sources, and to report foreign intelligence from those sources. The CIA has a system to produce operations officers who are experts in regions or issues. An ops officer who specializes in Southeast Asian Counter-terrorist operations, for example.

The CIA is uniquely positioned in foreign countries, has close and long-standing relationships with the local security services, including civilian and military intelligence, local police, and national police. The CIA has run hundreds, thousands of covert intelligence ops in foreign countries, with and without the cooperation of foreign services.

CIA officers are resident in the foreign country, some have studied the language, and all try to understand the cultural issues involved in working the foreign operating environment. The CIA has a large support structure at Langley, nearly totally focused on foreign operations.

FBI agents are trained, work on the job, are rewarded and promoted based on successful prosecution of criminals. The skills FBI agents develop are phenomenal—in America. Unfortunately, the FBI's law enforcement and prosecutorial approach applied in overseas CT environments, in my experience, is obstructive at best, and harmful to our national security at worst.

For example, I worked a CT operation post-9/11 in a foreign country, with the goal of disrupting or destroying a terrorist network that had killed, kidnapped, and brutalized numerous Americans and others. It was a complicated covert op involving input and assistance from numerous foreign government security organizations and officials, with whom the CIA worked very closely. The op took place away from the capital, in a desolate and remote area. I was the CIA officer on the ground, coordinating the complex moving pieces with the local intel, military, and police.

During the long op, we developed intel that a terrorist safehouse was a meeting and support site. Or it might be used to house the hostages themselves. The intel came about through careful and close cooperation between the CIA and our local allies. We each contributed our strengths. The CIA had technical means, guidance, and training to offer. The foreign services had in-depth cultural and linguistic knowledge, an existing network of contacts and sources, and a deep motivation to help their friends.

After careful planning, using multiple technical tools and sources, we coordinated a pre-dawn, lightning-quick raid of the safehouse. While the hostages were not present, there was a treasure trove of documents, cell phones, and computers, in addition to terrorist support staff. Our allies, in whose country, and under whose laws, we were working, took control of the detainees and material seized.

Gathered together, locals and CIA, at a military intel office, we discussed the best approach to processing the take, with the need for speed implicitly understood by all. We came up with a satisfactory division of responsibilities—locals take the documents in the local language and the detainees for interrogation, CIA take the laptops and cell phones for exploitation—when I got a call from CIA management.

Management let me know that the FBI agent who had flown in from the States the day before was on his way to the scene. I was to coordinate with him. As the officer in the field, my goal was to keep the FBI agent away from the ops, since he had a net zero to add, to any facet of the op. At the same time, I appreciated the need for the FBI to appear to be involved, as they were under much pressure from Washington for 9/11 failures. My plan was to let him sit in on discussions, keep him informed, but keep him away from the actual operations.

After 9/11, the FBI had been attempting to assert "primacy" in any situation that involved a "crime against an American citizen," no matter where that crime occurred in the world. In this case, the terrorists had kidnapped Americans. The same terrorists had kidnapped and murdered other Americans. So, this case was a perfect test bed for the FBI's new theory of primacy.

When the FBI agent arrived on scene, hours later, we had completed dividing responsibilities for the "take" from the safehouse. The FBI agent strode into the room, acting like he had just busted a ring of check-kiters in Milwaukee. He whipped out a roll of yellow crime scene tape from his bag, and wrapped the two piles of boxes and equipment with a criss-cross pattern of tape. He declared, "This is a crime scene. No one is to touch this evidence."

Our allies, their jaws on the floor, looked to me. All I could do was to call management. The CIA officers in charge there told me that Washington and the ambassador were trying to sort out lines of responsibility, and I should just let the FBI proceed with their duties. The FBI agent had the material wrapped and palletized, and he left on the next flight.

Mind reeling, I was forced to channel all my energies into keeping our allies from shooting the naïve FBI agent. Our local allies were enraged. Their men had fast-roped into the compound, their men had risked their lives for this take. Using every ounce of case-officering skills that I had, I was able to separate our allies from our mutual enemy, the FBI. With our allies in tow, I retreated to their offices for an all-nighter, trying to convince them that this had not been some sort of conspiracy to steal the take from them.

In the short run we were able to repel the FBI (they never showed their faces in the field again). We ran the op to a successful conclusion, but God only knows what ever happened to the take from that raid. None of those terrorists has ever been prosecuted in the USA. However, several of them became shark bait at the conclusion of the ops run by our allies. And an American hostage lives in freedom today, because of the CIA and foreign teamwork.

The FBI was designed to be, and is today, a US-based law enforcement agency. The CIA was designed to be, and is, a foreign-based intelligence and covert action agency. The 9/11 Commission, which was driven by those famous intelligence experts, the Jersey Girls, resulted in the creation of the DNI. It also resulted in a push for the FBI to be more involved in "intelligence."

The 9/11 Commission empowerment of the FBI's role in intelligence clouded what had been relatively clear lines of responsibility. The FBI, after 9/11, began pushing into foreign countries in unprecedented numbers and with aggressive outreach. They claimed any operation as their own if it involved a crime against a US citizen or person. The FBI pushed its agents overseas, with little to no training or experience. Agents from Little Rock, who had chased white collar criminals in Arkansas and Missouri, flew into embassies in the Middle East, Asia, and Africa to "investigate" terrorist "crimes."

In the aftermath of the PantiesBomber, FBI agents took control of the "crime scene" and the Nigerian detainee. At some point, the FBI read the Nigerian his rights. They put the terrorist in an American jail, and gave the Nigerian an American lawyer.

In the meantime, the bomber's terrorist trainers, planners, suppliers, funders, and other co-conspirators got advance warning upon his arrest, and avoided detection and capture. Not only was the ability of the bomber to obtain a seat on an American plane an intel failure, but the "law enforcement" handling of the incident, and the FBI's interrogation were also abject failures.

Coordination and communication among agencies in the GWOT are extremely important. But more important than that is the need for the right tool to be applied to a job. When an incident calls for a counter-terror, intelligence approach, that is what should be used. The dysfunctional hyper-bureaucracy created by the 9/11 Commission, including the DNI and the National Counter-terrorism Center (NCTC), should be scuttled. The President's "Terrorism Counsel" should be fired.

The solution for terrorist attacks on the homeland is a joint approach between the Department of Defense, and the CIA. The DoD is responsible for detaining enemy combatants. The CIA is responsible for interrogation and intelligence exploitation of enemy operatives and operations. Those two responsible agencies should call on other agencies for their specific skills, when needed. Until we return to a sane bureaucratic solution, America and its citizens will be endangered instead of protected.

Chapter 17
Obama, Osama, and Moammar

May 2011

Congratulations to Barack Obama and John Brennan. They evidently used the resources available to them to implement George W. Bush's policies in the Global War on Terror. A quick and lethal covert action followed a decade-long intelligence operation, that began with harsh CIA interrogations, and surely included massive use of all types of intelligence resources available—collection and analysis.

The Osama hit provides a glimpse into an unsettling reality. PC-Progressives like Obama always are loudly vocal in declaring their humaneness, and love for mankind. And they are loudly vocal in chastising evil conservatives for war-mongering and immoral use of covert action. Yet, when the PC-Progressives actually gain power, they become addicted to covert action.

Obama and his clique love covert operations. They've demonstrated that in the Global War on Terror (or "overseas contingency operations building bridges to Islamic extremists"). Instead of actually pursuing the war in Afghanistan with the tools in place—soldiers and Marines—they prefer Predator strikes in the hinterlands of Pakistan. The number of these covert action killings has soared from 2009 to 2011—with estimates of 5 dead in 2009 under Bush growing to several hundred dead in 2010 under Obama.

Because these are covert attacks, Obama and his clique don't have to acknowledge the facts. They can bluster and bloviate, and deny, appearing all things to all people. Their political base, the PC-Progressives, pretend they don't notice the carnage. The anti-terrorism side notices and tacitly approves. This having-your-cake-and-eating-it-too technique is pure PC-Progressivism. Their whole political philosophy is built on a foundation of lies.

Loving humanity while hating individual humans is the fundamental core of PC-Progressivism—which is a pure lie. Hating capitalism while reveling in the benefits of the American economy is living a lie. Babbling about "saving the earth" from carbon, all the while globe-trotting in a private jet is a lie. Standing up for "labor" while destroying entire industries with union goon-squads is a lie. Pick any PC-Progressive position, and you'll see that it is built on a lie.

So, the Obama clique's love of covert action is not surprising. However, those who care about the truth, the future of our country, and the health of our vital national security organizations should pay careful attention to the mendacious actions carried out in our name in Libya.

With a straight face, Obama declared that there were no "boots on the ground" in Libya. The next day his clique leaked the fact that CIA covert operators were on the ground. With a straight face, the Obama clique declared that our goal was not regime change, but rather humanitarian relief.

Within hours of that declaration, covert humanitarian action was unleashed on the Libyans. Humanitarian cruise missiles delivered humanitarian relief to Khadafy's residential compound.

The CIA leadership now is more political than ever. Never in its history has a pure political hack been in charge, before now. Never has an administration been so enamored of lying and hiding its true foreign policies behind covert action.

The Libyan operation has all the makings of a disaster for the CIA. In the Bay of Pigs operation, the Kennedy brothers inherited a plan already in motion, with covert teams in the process of training upon the Kennedys' arrival at the White

House. Careful planning for a covert invasion was already in motion. The Kennedys gave their approval to continue.

The Kennedys, much like Obama, were concerned about their image. Unlike Obama, at least the President had served in the military, and had some idea about combat operations. Even so, after approving the covert invasion, while denying there were boots on the ground to the public, the Kennedys ultimately lost their nerve. As communist Cubans massacred the CIA's invasion force on the ground in the Bay of Pigs, the indigenous commanders begged their CIA masters for air support.

The Kennedys pondered the emergency requests from Agency management, dithered, and finally denied the request. The invasion was crushed by overwhelming Cuban ground and air attacks. 1200 Cuban exiles of the invasion brigade were captured, scores died. The Kennedys' response was to demand more covert actions— assassination plans against Castro, spiraling into lunacy and tarnishing the CIA's reputation when revealed later.

The disaster inflicted on the Agency by the Kennedys began a cycle of degeneration that endured until 9/11. Successive administrations, with the exception of Ronald Reagan's, misused and abused the CIA, or at best neglected it. Only on September 12, 2001 did the Agency regain a mission. The CIA's refurbished reputation, as a result of GWOT successes, is now in jeopardy in Libya.

Of course, the CIA will not refuse orders from Obama's office to carry out covert action in Libya. But for anyone who understands the Bay of Pigs debacle, the political fallout, and the damage inflicted on the CIA, it is only right that we should fear the same damage and downward spiral from the upcoming Obama/Hillary Libyan covert action.

Chapter 18
John Brennan— Connecting the Dots Spells Conflict of Interest

Originally appeared on Parcbench.com; Jan. 12, 2010

On Christmas Day the now-infamous Panties Bomber spluttered into the headlines. Riding the coattails of a brave Dutchman, who actually put out the fire (did he extinguish the Nigerian panties too?), the Obama administration's answer to Janet Reno, Janet Napolitano, declared that her system had worked just fine.

The President, pausing from his rounds of tropical golf and topless body surfing, surfaced just long enough to tell his buddies on CNN and MSNBC that our charred crotch immigrant was just a lone wolf extremist, or he was "alleged" to be. Nothing to see here, move along. Then our intrepid President must have plunged back into the surf, or onto the fairway, secure in the knowledge that his words had calmed the seas, lowered the waters, cooled the planet, mollified Al-Qaeda, and soothed Kim Jong Il and the Iranians.

On further reflection, maybe his words were not quite enough. Maybe Americans had heard his throwaway lines one time too many. After the Christmas weekend, evidently in no particular hurry, our leader's aides seem to have realized that his teleprompter may have been loaded up with sweet nothings a little too quickly. He emerged from his paradise hideaway again on Monday.

After Janet N's incredible claims, Obama's handlers realized they had a Carter-sized problem on their hands. Immediately the President began the finger pointing.

Security and intelligence services had failed. Dropped the ball. Failed to connect the dots.

But wait, this is the most intelligent president in the history of the office. Surrounded by the most intelligent, savvy, industrious, earnest, sincere and helpful staff and cabinet ever. Plus ethical too. Our young president, buzz cut rapidly graying, had pledged that he would fix all the idiotic things that the dunce he replaced had screwed up.

Maybe Obama had just not yet gotten around to that "protecting the country from terrorists" item on his agenda. Maybe he thought that his Cairo speech had done the trick. Or maybe he thought that Al-Qaeda had just hated Bush, and that his famous mental muscle was better suited to really hard work, like health-care reform, global warming, choosing the teams for the Sweet 16, or picking a name for his next puppy.

Whatever the reason, Umar from Nigeria, by way of Amsterdam, on a Delta flight, got Obama's attention. And now Obama was primed to fix this whole "contingency" thing, or whatever he and Janet had decided to call terrorism. Whatever they called it, he and his Counter-terrorism advisor, John Brennan had assured us that we were NOT at war with it.

Americans must seem like a funny bunch of whiners to the President. Seemingly unaware, tone deaf, and blind to American concerns and lifestyles, Obama seemed stunned when he faced the press again, back in Washington, wearing a tie, 11 days after the terror attack. Thin and reedy, Obama read the text that declared that his intelligence and security services had utterly failed by allowing this attack to happen.

White House staff released a photo of Obama appearing to speak fiercely to his Cabinet before his speech. During the public speech, Obama declared his system a disastrous failure. Okay so far. But now his prescription: "I directed my Counter-terrorism advisor, John Brennan, to lead a thorough review into our terrorist watch-listing system so we can fix what went wrong."

Now Barack has wandered into deep denial of reality. Brennan, a George Tenet lackey, hooked his wagon to Obama's star early enough that he became the candidate's go-to-guy for intel matters during the campaign. Brennan rode that pony as far as it would go, until the rabid left-wing forced his boss to throw his nomination to run the CIA out the window, due to concerns about his role in "torture" (don't get me going on that issue).

Brennan, a consummate bureaucrat and career CIA analyst, had been the first director of the new "fusion centers" the 9/11 Commission required—first the Terrorist Threat Integration Center (TTIC) and then the National Counterterrorism Center (NCTC). Their main job was to connect those pesky dots that the IC missed prior to the 9/11 attack.

Brennan birthed dysfunctional twins, and left the government soon after. He became a dreaded contractor, cashing in for big bucks, and took the helm of a company that sold intel products and services. Who would his customer be? If you guessed NCTC, you'd be right.

And what might Mr. Brennan have been peddling to NCTC? A software system to connect the dots and manage the terrorist watchlist! When the time came to pay back Brennan for his dedication to the Obama campaign, "the most ethical administration in history" promptly issued an ethics waiver to Mr. Brennan. Don't worry, no conflicts of interest. Move along, nothing to see here.

Isn't it fun to watch sausage being ground? A bureaucracy created to fix a system that failed to connect the dots, led by Mr. Brennan, buys a system designed to connect the dots, sold by Mr. Brennan. When Brennan's bureaucracy using Brennan's system is declared an abject failure, the administration's solution is to have Mr. Brennan undertake an immediate investigation to connect the dots on the dot-connecting failure.

Nice work if you can get it. Any bets on what Mr. Brennan's findings will be? The summary findings will be made public later this week. Stay tuned. This could get interesting—sort of like a train wreck.

Chapter 19
Maghreb Mutinies: Karl Marx Meet Sayid Qutb; Lenin Meet Osama bin Laden

Originally appeared in: <u>BigPeace</u>, *January 28, 2011*

The Wikileaks revolutions sweeping the Arab world seem democratically promising. Tweeting twenty-somethings challenge iron-fisted dictators. Populist mutineers trash the ruling clique's Mediterranean villas. Royal families (and wannabe royal families) pack up their gold and flee to Europe or a nearby sympathetic kingdom. Popular sentiment in the North African countries ("the Maghreb," the lands beyond the sunset) appears to support reform. But it is a broad-based support—with a wide range of flavors. All the reformers, in all the Maghreb, share a commonality—they are Muslim.

Recent history provides a parallel to guide our understanding, and response, to the Maghreb Mutiny—the Russian Revolution.

A broad-based coalition reflecting popular discontent, made up of a spectrum of loosely linked groups that shared a common philosophical base. In Russia, the common base was socialism. In the Maghreb the common base is Islam.

The majority of people in 1905 Russia supported government reform to relieve the oppression of the tsar's royal dictates. A socialist coalition, ranging from the radical Marxists, to the more moderate Social Revolutionists, took control of the Russian government after the tsar fell to riots, strikes, and protests. The majority of people in the Maghreb support government reforms to relieve the oppression of their leaders' secular dictates. While details are sketchy in the Maghreb, it is very likely that the opposition is gathering a coalition, which will be formed around their common belief system—Islam. It is also sure that the Muslim coalition will represent a range of flavors—from modernist Islam, to Islamic extremists. The extremist Muslim Brotherhood, followers of the teachings of Sayid Qutb, and bin Laden followers are surely in the coalition. If, as has happened in Tunisia, and as it seems increasingly likely elsewhere, the Maghreb Mutinies succeed in overthrowing dictators, the aftermath could continue the parallels to the Russian revolution. This will not be a good development, for America, or for the people involved. After the broad-based Russian socialist revolution, a committed extremist minority, the communist Bolsheviks, out-maneuvered the majority. The communists were tireless in using political, military, and terror tactics to wear down their coalition partners. Finally, the Bolsheviks seized power from their coalition partners, in October 1917. The immediate aftermath was a bloodbath—the Red Terror. The Red Terror was followed by several years of ruthless civil war. The communists wiped out their coalition partners and anyone else who resisted their rule. The next 70 years were miserable, bloody, soul-deadening proof of the bankruptcy of communism. While we may cheer a seemingly democratic uprising in the Maghreb, to paraphrase the prophet Hosea, the sowers of the wind shall reap the whirlwind. The fall of secular oppressors could very likely lead to the rise of religious oppressors, even against the will of the majority. A Green Terror could very easily mimic the Red Terror.

Marxist extremists did it in Russia; Qutubist extremists could repeat the strategy and tactics in the Maghreb.

If ever America needed a self-interested, strong, clear voice in the realm of foreign affairs, now is the time. Unfortunately, we are saddled with the reed- thin, apologetic Obama foreign affairs crowd. Following Obama's Cairo apology to the Muslim world, he withdrew to the golf course on Ft. Myers.

His Middle East representatives, czar George Mitchell, and foreign affairs neophyte (which part of first lady of Arkansas prepared her for international affairs?) Hillary Clinton, are doomed to disrespect in a region where face and power are requirements for effectiveness.

Will we sit back and watch the second coming of an extremist coup following a popular revolution, dooming to slavery the masses struggling for freedom? Or will we aid and abet the wrong side? The President's shaky foundation--apologizing for America, and uncertain bows to kings—does not bode well for America's interests.

Prepare for the whirlwinds.

Chapter 20
North Korea: President Obama, Time to Be a Leader

Originally appeared in: <u>BigPeace</u>; *Nov. 24, 2010*

The two remaining members of the Axis of Evil, Iran and North Korea, have made clear their lack of respect for our callow and shallow President, as he traipsed around the world with his gold-plated posse in tow.

Tehran continues its march towards production of nuclear weapons just as fast as Russia, North Korea, and rogue suppliers of technology can feed them resources.

Meanwhile, North Korea manipulated American scientists to reveal the advanced stages of their nuclear weapons production facilities. And just in case Obama was on the golf course, or flying to a ceremony in Europe, and didn't hear that message, the communist Koreans on Tuesday carpet-shelled a free Korean island.

Can you hear them now, Mr. Obama? Do you realize that it wasn't President Bush that they hate? Do you realize how ridiculous they consider you? Do you realize how much you have humiliated the country that you chose to call home? Do you realize that America is the vanguard of good in the world?

The Axis of Evil are not humane. They are not humanitarian. They are not caring. They are not fair. They are not free. They are not open. They are not dedicated to human decency, liberty, or the pursuit of happiness.

They are dedicated to control. Control of their own people. Control of you. Control of me. For what purpose?

For evil, Mr. Obama. They are evil. Their goals are evil. Their intent is evil. They mask their goals in ideology—religious (Iran's theocracy) or quasi-religious (North Korea's worship of its leader and his spawn). But their ultimate goal is to control.

You kow-tow to kings, despots, and tyrants. Bullies sense weakness. Bullies sense cowardice. The Axis of Evil are bullies. Your actions since inauguration signal weakness and cowardice. Allies, foes, and potential foes all around the world hear and see your message of weakness. They smell blood in the water.

It is clear that you have neither the experience nor aptitude to undertake the job which you won in 2008. But you could show your character. Fire your team. Then resign. Allow leaders with experience and wisdom to make the hard decisions required to keep our country and its allies safe and free.

The whole world is watching. China is intrigued. Russia awaits. Do the right thing, for America.

Part Three

Military Obliteration

Chapter 21
Libya: Obama's Progressively Flexible War

Originally published: BigPeace, September 15, 2011

Unprecedented is putting it mildly. Never before in the history of the United States of America have we acted so duplicitously in foreign affairs. A strong ally in the global war on terror, Libya's former strongman, Moammar al-Gaddafi, renounced his weapons of mass destruction program after he saw our resolve and military power in Afghanistan and Iraq. He surrendered two terrorist suspects for trial. From an international pariah state, to a strong partner in the terror war, Gaddafi was a tiger who changed his stripes, joining America in its war on terror.

What was his reward for nearly a decade of cooperation with us? An American-led revolution. The Obama-Hillary clique called their little revolution a NATO mission to insure human rights. Nice word-smithing by the PC-Progressive war-mongers.

Call it what you will, Hillary and her estrogen-drunk cabal at State dragged the US into a civil war (President Obama: "No American boots on the ground."). The height of the duplicity by the PC-Progressives in this unprecedented American-led war might best be measured by comparing the ravings of the same PC-Progressives against the wars that George Bush led. Let's look at some of the PC-Progressive rants against Iraq and Afghanistan:

"No blood for oil." Remember that quaint PC – Progressive chant during the Iraq War? Well, in case you haven't noticed the Libyan war really is blood for oil. We're tangled up in Europe's green nightmare. They don't have enough oil. Windmills and solar are a joke. They need oil. Libya sits on huge reserves. Solution? Blood for oil! Only problem is, the blood is spilled for oil shipments to Italy and France.

"It's a civil war." Democrats demanded that the US withdraw from Iraq because "it is now a civil war." Well, the Libyan war has been a civil war from the first Obama-launched cruise missile to the latest strike on a Gaddafi compound. A civil war in Libya is okay, but one in Iraq is not?

"Arrogance." Obama's teleprompter told him one time to say that Bush was arrogant, dismissive, even derisive toward our allies. Sending volleys of cruise missiles down an ally's chimneys is probably as arrogant, dismissive and derisive as you can get.

"No exit strategy." Remember the Progressive geniuses who constantly chided the Bush administration and its dunces for not foreseeing every twist and turn as the Iraq and Afghanistan wars unfolded? Many of them are now in the Obama-Hillary administration. Yes, the same administration that has just realized that the "freedom fighters" they've supported in Libya are actually al-Qaeda linked Islamic extremists. "We'll thump Gaddafi and then let al-Qaeda take over." How's that for an exit strategy?

"Cowboy Bush going it alone." PC-Progressives moaned and whined constantly that President Bush was a rogue international operator, invading Iraq alone, with no international support. In fact, Bush assembled a multi-national force in Iraq, made up of units from dozens of countries. The multi-national force held daily press briefings to provide details of operations. The Libyan operation is cloaked in secrecy and the legacy media erected a wall of silence to protect Obama-Hillary. No details leak out about the foreign forces involved in the civil war. Foreign troops are invisible. Even the composition of the Libyan rebels has been cloaked by the media. Only now do the media dare to report mujahedeen in the ranks.

"Dumb war." During his stint at a state senator, Barack said, "I don't oppose all wars... What I am opposed to is a dumb war." The wise international theorist from Illinois then went on to derisively call Bush's experts "weekend warriors" who arrogantly shoved "their own ideological agendas down our throats, irrespective of the costs in lives lost and in hardships borne." Now that Obama sits on the throne in the West Wing, the whole weekend warrior issue is passé. Obama's geniuses, Hillary Clinton, Susan Rice, and Samantha Power, between them don't even qualify as weekend warriors. More like a sorority rush hit squad. And their ideological agenda? It's not clear that they are weighing lives lost and hardships borne in their mad dash to destabilize North Africa.

"War crimes, human rights violations." PC-Progressives constantly filled the airwaves of NPR, ABC, NBC and the other legacy media, as well as the digital pipes at Huffington Post with allegations of American war crimes and violations of human rights in Iraq. In Libya, based on public reporting, there seem to be no human rights violations, only clean hits on military objectives.

"Pre-emptive strikes are unconstitutional, against international law." The chorus of PC-Progressives calling for Bush's impeachment, Rumsfeld's arrest for war crimes, and Cheney's immediate execution for crimes against humanity rose to a crescendo during the Iraq invasion. The mere idea of an "aggressive war," attacking a helpless nation before it attacked us, was deemed "Hitlerian." Well, how does that little mustache look on Obama's lip? Obama-Hillary justified the massive air-strikes against Gaddafi on humanitarian grounds. Regardless, Gaddafi had not attacked America. Obama's Libyan war is a perfect example of a pre-emptive strike.

There is more hypocrisy in the Libyan desert, but you get the drift. Just as their American ideological forefathers executed perfect 180's when the Stalin-Hitler non-aggression pact dissolved as Nazi tanks stormed Russia, American PC-Progressives today neatly "pivot" in their disdain for war, bombs, missiles, death, human rights, non-aggression, international understanding, and all their other petty attacks against Normal Americans.

When the American military, commanded by Normal Americans, acts for American interests, the Obama-Hillary clique were against the actions. When the American military, commanded by PC-Progressives, attacks in support of unclear internationalist interests, PC-Progressives are all for a little death and destruction. Selective Progressive Outrage—sounds like a mental disease.

Chapter 22
War-time Priorities—Tilting at Lavender Windmills

Originally published: BigPeace, December 8, 2010

We are a nation at war. We are engaged in combat in two countries. We have combat and support troops in scores of countries around the globe. Hostile groups plan and operate 24 hours a day against us. They would love to get their hands on an American to take hostage. They would love to pull off a Mumbai attack in downtown San Francisco.

Our enemies plot ways to weaken our economy and our society. Chinese espionage agents actively steal our economic secrets. Russian espionage officers run networks under commercial cover, are arrested, and then whisked out of the country in a 10 for 2 swap. The Russians muscle us into a new nuclear arms treaty.

A rogue Aussie cyber-punk operating a global intelligence collection network, with funding from who knows where, recruits penetrations of our military and diplomatic services. His recruits provide him with hundreds of thousands of classified government communications. He brazenly flaunts American security, and publishes his espionage haul on the internet, and shares the raw take with a variety of hostile news outlets, including the New York Times.

An insane punk Communist dictatorship in Korea teases and taunts American good will. After taking millions in assistance funds in exchange for quitting its nuclear weapons development programs, North Korea missiles an allied ship. Then, rubbing our nose in its mess, the little commie-state shells an allied island into oblivion.

Tin pot Latin American communist dictatorships flaunt their disdain for American leadership.

And what is the Progressive Obama administration's national security focus? Ensuring that homosexuals have equal rights to join and serve in America's all-volunteer military. Obama's campaign to end "Don't ask, don't tell" is pay-back to his rabid homosexual and Progressive base.

We have had more killed in action in Afghanistan in 2010 than during the eight years previously. We are still battling terrorist and insurgent forces in Iraq. We have combat troops across the globe. We are assisting multiple countries around the world in counter-terrorism operations.

Our military resources are thin in many areas. We need many more linguists—Dari, Pashto, Arabic, and Farsi. We need technical skills—computers and communications. We need people who can operate in foreign cultures.

But in all of the far-flung places we are operating, against various enemies, and with various allies, there has not been one public report of our military not having enough homosexuals to get the job done. I have not heard of an unmet demand for open homosexuals in our forward operating bases in Afghanistan.

Our military should be doing exactly what we need to do to win our wars. Our military should be doing exactly what we need to do to support American and allied interests abroad. Our military is not the place for Politically Correct attacks on our culture.

Those who, during our prosecution of a global war, waste one second of one military member's time on a social issue, come very close to being a friend of our enemies. One general, one private, one sailor, one airman, any single military member who wastes one minute dealing with the Obama administration's, and their Pelosite friends' corrosive drive to allow open homosexuals to serve in the military, is wasting American military resources. Those resources could be used to eliminate the Taliban. Instead, our military is forced to waste massive amounts of time and energy tilting at social engineering windmills.

Stop the cultural combat. Leave the military alone. Let them fight. Let them win. Anything less is near treason.

Chapter 23
Negotiations with the Taliban—Foreign Affairs and Eggheads

Originally published: BigPeace, October 25, 2010

Obama wants to negotiate with the Taliban? What sort of brilliant strategist devised that idea? I'll see your Jones, and raise you a Hillary.

Not since the waning days of the Johnson administration has America had so many clueless eggheads deciding the course of our history. A holdover from Kennedy's presidency, National Security Advisor McGeorge Bundy, was a liberal shining star. Much like Obama's geniuses, it seems that his credentials were based on high aptitude test scores. He also talked Harvard into hiring him as a professor holding only a B.A. degree, and was at 27 the youngest dean of the faculty at Harvard. He was the Chairman of Johnson's 303 Committee, the U.S. government's covert action coordinating group. He played a leading role in such Democrat fiascoes as the Bay of Pigs, bombing North Vietnam, covert operations in Cambodia, the Cuban missile crisis, and more.

The next convocation of self-proclaimed geniuses inflicted on us was the Carter administration. His National Security Advisor, Zbigniew Brzezinski, oversaw Carter's bowing and scraping to the Evil Empire, the communist Russians. The combination of Carter's sweater-clad misunderstanding of our adversaries and Brzezinski's self-aggrandizing showboating caused foreign affairs disasters, one after another. The Soviets picked our pockets in the strategic missile negotiations. They then head-faked

Carter and invaded Afghanistan while the brilliant, populist Democrat rhapsodized about world peace and understanding. And, in a humiliating slap heard around the world, Iranian Islamic extremist revolutionaries seized our embassy in Tehran, and kidnapped 66 American citizens. But the humiliation was not over for the Democrat geniuses. The Carter White House micromanaged a Delta force rescue attempt that fizzled out in the Iranian desert. It ended in disaster and eight brave Americans lost their lives.

With Democrat geniuses again running our foreign affairs and combat, we should refresh our memory of the consequences of following the advice of "brilliant" liberal technocrats. The results include the Bay of Pigs, restricted rules of engagement in Vietnam, body counts, hearts and minds, SALT II, Afghanistan, an entire American embassy seized and held hostage, dead soldiers in sandstorms. And now we have the reprise of Johnson/Carter brain trusts— the Obama clique of professors. Can their brilliance possibly produce different outcomes than the previous Ivy League Democrat bozos?

So far, Obama's crowd has produced, among other foreign affairs coups, the "closure" of Gitmo. The persecution of CIA officers for interrogating terrorists. The elevation of gays in the military to a policy level issue while we conduct two wars. Confused incoherence on handling terrorist prisoners of war—a plan, decided at breakfast, to prosecute combatants captured on the battlefield for felonies in U.S. courts. Hit with a massive terrorist attack by an al-Qaeda penetration agent in the U.S. Army— Obama and his geniuses warned against connecting the dots to come to any conclusions. Obama's National Counterterrorism Advisor investigated himself after both his previous CIA analytical program and his commercial program, which he sold to his former office, failed. The same geniuses were unable to "connect the dots" to identify the Panties Bomber. The muddled undergraduate seminar to choose a strategy in Afghanistan. The muddled strategy that resulted—Obama announced a withdrawal date at the same time he announced a surge. The panicked firing of a military professional after a liberal hit piece reveals that, wait—he thought Joe Biden was an idiot! The elevation to the status of military savior of the general who the progressives, led by Obama and Hillary, derided as a lying traitor. Nation-building in Afghanistan. Rolling over for the Russians after the FBI arrested ten, count 'em ten, covert agents and agent handlers living and working as "illegals" in the U.S. North Korea blew up a South Korean ship. Iran fired up its nuclear reactors, with Russian expertise, after liberal analysts and the Obamaites assured us that the Iranians had no such ability, desire or expertise. A unilateral declaration of the end of combat in Iraq, while Americans continue to fight and die there. And there are more. Billy Joel could do a new "We didn't light the fire" song with just Obama's blunders.

Foreign affairs disasters, miscalculations, blunders, mistakes, crises, call them what you will. For anyone who cares about American interests the last two years were horrific.

So, back to negotiating with the Taliban. Why? The only reason the Taliban would negotiate with us is to buy time. They know we are leaving. They even know the date. Obama told them. They have all the time in the world. They just wait until Obama turns tail and declares an end to combat. Then we leave. Then the massacres begin.

Anyone old enough to remember the fall of Saigon? I worked in a refugee camp, more than ten years after Saigon fell. The destroyed lives, shattered families, ruined bodies, spirits and minds trickled out of Vietnam into the camps. Millions of people risked life and limb to escape the totalitarian, anti-American regime that murdered, tortured, or re-educated anyone who had contact with Americans.

What is different in Afghanistan? When Obama declares combat over, will the Taliban be merciful to Afghan women who worked with Americans? How about the Afghan Army and intelligence service? Will the Taliban accept the police? Recent history suggests that there will be a bloodbath worse than Vietnam. The Khmer Rouge in Cambodia exterminated nearly a third of their fellow countrymen. And they were only motivated by politics, not religion. Obama's geniuses could potentially have the blood of millions on their hands. Professorial seminars and 99th percentile SATs could prove to be deadly—again.

Chapter 24
Ministry of Truth Declaration: Combat is Assistance

Originally published: BigPeace, September 10, 2010

American troops on an Iraqi Army base in Baghdad laid down heavy "assistance" fire with their "assistance" M4's last week. Despite Barack Obama's stone-faced declaration that US military forces in Iraq are not actually "combat" troops, our combat troops did what they do best—engaged in combat with the enemy.

Linguistic parlor games are probably amusing in the Harvard Law Review lounge. Young Barack (Have you heard? He's the most intelligent editor ever!) likely engaged in heavy rhetorical combat with his peers and betters in the academy. His University of Chicago law classes are said to have been heavy on verbal class warfare, and tongue-lashing of American oppressors.

While it may have earned him brownie points at Columbia, in Chicago and at Cambridge, the young President's latest rhetorical sophistry is a deadly piece of self-delusion. His word games blatantly disrespect the real combat troops who are in Iraq, engaging in, or under constant threat of, combat. Under his putative command, these troops saw their unit names change overnight, magically creating Assist troops out of combat troops.

According to a reliable source, currently serving in Baghdad, soldiers there joke that the M1A1 is now the Main "Assist" Tank. Its 120mm gun is notorious for the assistance it provides. While grunts have always been cynical and are champion complainers, the blatant word games played by their commander-in-chief are sticking in the dog-faces' craws.

The source is currently engaged in infantry-to-infantry training of the Iraqi Army. He reports that from the perspective on the ground in Iraq, it appears they are re-living Vietnam, but this time in reverse. American involvement in Vietnam began with an advise and assist mission, and worked up to massive combat, prior to an ignominious, politically charged withdrawal. Now the Army is reliving that process backwards. From a massive combat mission, with no holds barred, to advise and assist, followed by an ignominious, politically charged withdrawal--it's déjà vu from '72.

With no workable government in sight, separatist sentiments growing in at least three enclaves, and weak-kneed counter-factual political pronouncements from the clique in Washington, the future is none too bright for Iraq. In the meantime, the future is clouded and dangerous for our "Assist" troops in Iraq.

Would that we had a real commander-in chief who could call on experience outside of the faculty lounge, the grad student gab-fest, or a campaign rally to inform his decisions. Lives are at stake. American honor is on the line. Yet liberal Newspeak emanates from the White House. What next? War is Peace? Ignorance is Strength? Where's the Ministry of Truth when you really need it?

Part Four

Global War on Terror
(uh, "contingency operations")

Chapter 25

"Good War" Counter-Insurgency Rx— Colonize or Come Home

Originally published: _September 1, 2010_

President Obama on Tuesday declared Iraq a done deal. Okay, he didn't support the surge, back in the Bush days. He and his anti-war pals in the Senate declared the war lost years ago. His liberal upbringing won't allow him to admit that a Republican president could possibly have been right. And yet, the architect of the surge, and stability, as it were, in Iraq, is now Obama's uniform in chief in the "Good War."

If one believed in omens, the future of our involvement in Afghanistan would not bode well. General David Petraeus, before he was demoted to replace General Stanley McChrystal, collapsed during Congressional testimony on the Obama strategy. Then General McChrystal was surgically removed by a left-wing media strike. If it was his campaign, Alexander the Great might have reconsidered his course, and visited the Oracle in Siwa again.

The President and his Progressive handlers declared our military efforts in Afghanistan "the Good War" to differentiate it from that numbskull Bush's "Bad War" in Iraq. After playing his anti-Bush card in the first weeks of his administration, Obama then called together all his geniuses to devise his Good War strategy.

Obama's geniuses developed a strategy that looks a lot like the Bush/Rumsfeld surge in Iraq. Except the geniuses revealed their end game before they even sat down to begin playing. Obama announced the target date for withdrawing US forces from Afghanistan, in the same teleprompted address that he announced the deployment.

The Taliban, Al-Qaeda, and their allies must have been confused. They surely must have thought this was some sort of elaborate ruse on the part of the geniuses. It didn't take them long to figure out, however, that the geniuses were not very good poker players. They actually had revealed their final plan. At least it appears so, up to today. Maybe the good general collapsed after contemplating the lack of exits in the rat hole in which he is trapped.

Obama's genius seminar on Afghanistan strategy was described by a White House aide as an attempt to avoid a "rush to war." Maybe the geniuses didn't notice that we had been at war in Afghanistan for more than half a decade before the thinker-in-chief was inaugurated.

As the afterglow of the media's near-orgasmic lovefest with Obama fades, it's time for an honest consideration of our Afghanistan policy and strategy. We are past the hunt for Osama. We are past the point of destroying Al-Qaeda's strongholds in the Hindu Kush. The Obama genius cabal has announced its goals as: "reverse the Taliban's gains, and promote a more capable and accountable Afghan government."

In layman's terms, what they plan is counter-insurgency and nation-building. Setting aside the difficulty of building a cohesive nation from the troubled ethnic mix within Afghanistan's present borders, let's just look at counter-insurgency.

There are many examples of previous successful and unsuccessful attempts at counter-insurgency. An honest consideration of our current goal in Afghanistan requires a review of both the successes and failures. Let's examine the common features of the successful counter-insurgencies, and the common features of the counter-insurgency failures. There may well be lessons for our efforts in Afghanistan. Southeast Asia offers a student of counter-insurgency at least three object lessons.

The United States' most striking success in counter-insurgency was the Moro Rebellion in the Philippines. The

US's only long-term foreign colony was the island nation of the Philippines, seized from Spain after the Spanish-American war. We occupied and ruled the Philippines as a colony from 1898 until after World War II.

The Muslim population in the Southern Philippines (the Moros) rebelled against American colonial authority. The Moro Rebellion was a classic counter-insurgency, with native fighters fading into the local population, and into the jungle, emerging to terrorize civilians and American soldiers alike. The American army, steeled by the Indian wars in the western US, was familiar with this style of warfare. They crushed the rebellion. During the counter-insurgency, the Moro territory was ruled by American military governors and their staff. Local elders and chiefs were consulted and brought into the government under the Americans' direct rule.

Total control of the civil, military, and economic reins of the Philippines set the stage for effective counter-insurgency operations. Total control, with relatively benign colonial rule, combined with harsh and punitive military attacks against insurgents, combined to convince the Moros to capitulate. After more than 12 years of insurgency, the American military turned over control of Moroland to a civilian US colonial government. And within a few decades, American colonial government came to a peaceful end, with an orderly transition to Philippine independence.

A solid counter-insurgency drove communists from Malaya, a British colony now independent Malaysia, in the years after WWII. Known in Britain and Malaysia as "The Emergency," a Chinese-led communist insurgency threatened the soon-to-be-independent colony.

The communists mostly ethnic Chinese were supported by Red China. They operated from bases within the impenetrable jungles down the spine of the Malay Peninsula. They had scant support from the populace, and waged a terror campaign against the British and innocent civilians.

The British colonial governing infrastructure permeated Malayan society down to the smallest village. Courts, police, governors, mayors, and all other reins of power were firmly in the hands of experienced British colonial administrators. Fair and just, but firm and swift, British justice permeated the colony. Military units, a mixture of British and locals, as well as units from other colonies, like the Ghurkas from Nepal, operated from colonial garrisons.

At the height of the insurgency, British and Malayan military units perfected the Special Forces model of operations the US military uses today. Targeted by aggressive intelligence operations, quick strikes on unsuspecting rebels devastated the communists. With total control of the country, the British colonials were able to stamp out any hint of localized support for the rebels. Within twelve years, the communists were routed and soundly defeated. The British turned over the colony to self-rule near the end of the Emergency.

Another highly successful counter-insurgency occurred in Hungary in 1956. Hungary was occupied by the Soviet Union after WWII. After a typical communist charade of free elections, the Hungarian government became a de facto colony of the Soviet Union. The USSR controlled the government and its economic and security policies. After six years of crushing Soviet communist domination, proud Hungarians, prodded by American covert action, began demonstrating against the communists. The demonstrations quickly spun out of control, and became a full-fledged insurgency, with fierce urban guerilla warfare. The Soviets responded with an invasion in force. Their total domination of the entire country, administratively, militarily, and economically, crushed the insurgency in less than two months.

The American experience with counter-insurgency in Vietnam is an interesting negative example. The US placed severe restrictions on its military operations against the combined forces of indigenous and foreign communist guerillas. In the post-colonial era, the US was wary of charges of neo-colonialism. America allowed the South

Vietnamese to run the government fueled by American dollars. Much like today in Afghanistan, American advisors looked on in helpless frustration. Corruption and in-fighting severely weakened social, economic, and military infrastructure throughout the country. America's counter-insurgency was doomed from the start. Without control of the political and economic infrastructure, military operations were unable to gain traction.

The Kennedys attempted to avoid the sure condemnation by the media that would come with an overt colonial-style imposition of government on their Vietnamese client-state. Instead, they tried to use covert action. They approved a coup against the ruling Diem family, which resulted in the murder of the Vietnamese President and his family. That bungled attempt at colonial power mongering spoiled the Kennedys' appetite for further meddling. A constant turnover of civilian and military rule in the Vietnamese government followed, with some governments lasting only weeks. With no foundation to support itself, the civilian population was left to its own devices. Although American military and civilian forces kept working to defeat the communist insurgency, the slow-motion collapse of the South Vietnamese government doomed the counter-insurgency.

These examples of counter-insurgency operations reveal a broad outline of the requirements for success. They also reveal the conditions that ensure failure of counter-insurgency operations.

Full-blown colonial control of a country's political, economic, and legal infrastructure provides a solid foundation to wage a successful counter-insurgency. The campaigns against indigenous forces in Malaya, the Moroland, and Hungary demonstrate the requirements for crushing such indigenous enemies. The template of requirements includes: complete colonial-style control of the contested country and full control of the political, military, and economic infrastructure of the country.

On the other hand, America's war in Vietnam is a template for failure in operations against indigenous insurgents. First, we did not maintain full control of the contested nation during the hostilities. The American administration attempted to use covert action to cloak its hand in controlling the client-state's government. Finally, civilians placed severe restrictions on military operations against the insurgents and their masters in North Vietnam.

Comparing these templates with Petreaus' dizzying task in Afghanistan reveals a near perfect match with the template for failure. We do not control the government infrastructure. President Karzai fired his pro-American Interior Minister, and intel chief. We do not control the economy or military. We have placed ourselves in a subordinate role, pretending that this is an Afghan problem, and we are just advisors. We hide behind a "coalition" of NATO and other allies, which make up a tiny fraction of forces, but complicate the operations exponentially. We have placed restrictions on our military actions (how about a medal for "courageous restraint"?). We undertake covertly actions which the President loudly decried during his campaign (targeted killings).

In Afghanistan, we stand at a crossroads—there are three possible paths ahead. Annexing Afghanistan as an American colony will lead to success and honor in the long run, with short term international condemnation. Maintaining the current status quo can only lead to inglorious defeat in both the short and long runs. Draw-down and withdrawal could also be an honorable conclusion, except for blame that will be heaped on us for the certain political and social failures that follow in the wake of our exit.

With Obama declaring an end to Iraq, maybe his much-vaunted genius will come up with a solution to Afghanistan. The choices are clear for anyone who examines the realities of COIN: Full-blown colonial power; half-hearted attempts at politically-correct advise-and-equip; or cut-and-run. Obama and his geniuses asked for the job. The new Republican Congress, with hearings and oversight, should keep us out of too much trouble. It should be an interesting two years.

Chapter 26
Counter-insurgency—Lessons from a Professional in the Philippines, Frontlines of the Global War on Terror

Originally appeared in <u>BigPeace</u>; Aug. 23, 2010

©Kent Clizbe

Demonstration of martial arts—Marine Basic Trainees

The Marine officer is compact and solid. He wears his combat fatigues pressed, with a neat crease in the upper sleeve. His buzz-cut is sharp and clean. His clear eyes, open expression, and intense gaze evidence intelligence and keen perception, softened by his baby face. A better specimen of Marine warrior is not likely to be found. But just a minute, this Marine is not in Jacksonville, or Twenty-nine Palms. This fighter in the Global War on Terror (GWOT) is a lieutenant in the Philippine Marine Corps (PMC). 1Lt. Romulo Dimayuga is taking part in a demonstration of Marine tactics at the PMC training base in Ternate, Cavite, south of Manila.

©Kent Clizbe

1Lt. Romulo Dimayuga who led anti-ASG combat patrol that killed Kaddafi Janjalani

Dimayuga led a platoon of Marines on a combat mission against a superior force of Abu Sayyaf Group (ASG) combatants. Weeks after he returned from the jungle with the remnants of his patrol (more than 50% of his men were killed or wounded in the battle, and Dimayuga still carries a bullet in his belly) he learned that his Marines had killed the then-leader of the ASG, Kaddafy Janjalani.

Kaddafy Janjalani

Overlooking Manila Bay, with a stunning view of the WWII American and Filipino positions defending the Japanese onslaught at Corregidor, with the Bataan peninsula looming in the far distance, the Filipino Marine base is nestled in a series of coves chiseled into the volcanic ridges of Luzon Island. The Marines conduct their Basic training for enlisted, and indoctrination training for officers in this rugged terrain.

Phil-Marine Force Recon practice beach assaults in view of Corregidor and Bataan

Commandant of the PMC, Major General Juancho Sabban, chatted with me during a break in the training demonstration. We talked about the Filipino military's successes in their hot war against the Al-Qaeda-linked ASG in the southern Philippines. He also commented on the theory and application of Counter-Insurgency (COIN) strategy, based on his time in command in Sulu Province.

©Kent Clizbe

Maj. Gen. Juancho Sabban

Sabban, a veteran of numerous combat operations against ASG and Moro Liberation Front (MILF) fighters in the Muslim regions of the Philippines, spent a good portion of his military career stationed in the South. During much of that time, he was in active combat operations. His first star was earned battling the ASG in Sulu.

The anti-terrorist, anti-insurgency military operations in the southern Philippines are similar in many ways to the COIN operations the US military is undertaking in Afghanistan today. Filipino troops face a violent insurgent threat in a tribal-based society in remote border regions inhabited by Islamic cultures that value highly warfare against outsiders and infidels.

The battle for hearts and minds, in Sulu, however, has been, arguably, much more effective than the battle in the Afghanistan-Pakistan frontier. General Sabban explained that his COIN operation, including working hand in hand with American units and civilian partners, is heavy on infrastructure development. Sabban said he was asked by an American Congressional delegation, which had been critical of the military operations, to provide a wish-list for funding. The Congressman was surprised to see that Sabban's list was not military equipment, but instead was requests for pumps, docks, roads, schools, wells, and other infrastructure to improve the lives of the inhabitants.

Sabban said that his country's COIN strategy was making good progress, with a few steps forward for every step back, like the recent suicide bombing at the Zamboanga airport. Upon reflection, he shared his belief that the difference between his COIN operations, and America's faltering progress in Afghanistan could be due to a difference in the political landscape of the southern Philippines and Afghanistan.

Sabban and I discussed the difference between complete control of an area, politically, economically, militarily, as the Republic of the Philippines enjoys in Sulu, and the U.S. situation in Afghanistan. While the U.S. must contend with a morally bankrupt, corrupt, ineffective and inept Afghan government, in order to win support from NATO and other allies, the Philippines owns the territory of its battle in Sulu. Although the island chain is nominally a part of the Autonomous Region of Muslim Mindanao, the Philippine government is the ultimate power, officially and in reality.

With no need to pretend that the locals are in control, and no need to make a show of local buy-in with either military or social operations, the PMC and its Filipino military brethren, are free to operate as necessary. But the most important ingredient is operating in a way that earns the respect of the populace. That requires exhibiting strength and manliness, maybe more than America is prepared to display publicly. The Muslim tribal culture respects adversaries and overlords who are strong and, to some extent, ruthless. That's right—sometimes hearts and minds follow where the short-hairs are led. The approach must be determined by the target culture, not by the aggressor culture.

©Kent Clizbe

Force Recon Marines discuss results of exercise

Only with culturally aware, socio-politico-economic-military total control of an insurgent region can a true COIN battle for hearts and minds be successful. As the United States proved nearly a hundred years ago, on the same ground that Filipino and American forces stand side by side in the Global War on Terror in Mindanao and Sulu today, complete colonial-style control of an insurgent territory is necessary for the success of COIN operations.

Epilogue

Tribute to an American Leader

Ronald Reagan—Inspiration for Personal Development

BigPeace, *February 2011*

The first Presidential election I was old enough to vote was 1980, Ronald Reagan's first successful run. My journey during his two terms was a miracle—from a lost anti-American liberal to a proud American veteran and conservative. Was that a coincidence? Or was it leadership?

I was a 20 year old, maggot-infested, long-haired, skull-full-of-mush product of liberal brain-washing. I read Time magazine every week, and watched Walter Cronkite on the 6 o'clock news. I'd spent twelve years in National Education Association controlled public schools. I knew that Joseph McCarthy was bad, that Richard Nixon had done something really bad and was "Tricky."

I knew that it was cool to "party." That drinking and marijuana were ways to open your mind and show how counter-culture you were. I knew that Ronald "Raygun-zzzz," like they pronounced it on the Woodstock album, was a whacky old kook.

As I looked for my voter registration card, I couldn't have cared less about the vote. I had no appreciation of my country, my freedom, or the grave responsibility that our country entrusted me with—the right to vote.

Drinking a six-pack every night, everything was pretty much a fog to me. I'd screwed up, big time, flunked out of college. Now I waited for the date to report to Air Force basic training. Riding my ten-speed over the Roanoke

River, up the hill to Gaston for a four hour shift in the mini-mart a couple times a week kept me busy.

Faced with the momentous decision, Jimmy Carter, or Ronald Reagan, I threw away my vote. Thank God I didn't vote for Carter, but I didn't vote for Reagan either. Something I'd read in National Lampoon stuck with me when I went to the fire station that day, and I wrote in "Nobody." What a waste.

Basic training in San Antonio started a week after President Reagan's inauguration, the end of January 1981. Sobered up, I started a slow progression to reality. Basic whipped a little discipline into me. Vietnamese language training and technical training showed me that I could learn, and had a talent for languages, and a passionate interest in Asia.

Three years in the Philippines kept my interest in Asia alive, and opened my eyes to the beauty of America.

Discharged and back in college, it was President Reagan's second term. Of course, I'd voted for the Gipper the second time around, fully aware and sober.

Being a veteran in a university, during the long peaceful Cold War interregnum, was eye-opening. I saw the liberal bias and vile anti-Americanism on campus, directed at President Reagan.

Ronald Reagan was my hero now. He stood up to the communists, who I now understood, after studying the Vietnam war, and communism, were exactly what President Reagan called them—evil. And he stood up to the American friends of the communists, the Progressives, liberals—Carter, the Kennedys, McGovern, Jesse Jackson, and the press.

Every day, I realized more and more how right President Reagan was, in foreign policy and in domestic policy. By 1989, when President Reagan left office, I was teaching at a university in Saudi Arabia, after working in a refugee camp in Southeast Asia.

Every day, I thanked God I was an American, and that my country was a shining beacon of hope, freedom, and prosperity for the world. I was proud to be a Reagan American.

Ronald Reagan, reviled by the Progressive haters, and denigrated by the liberal press, was the ideal of American humility, humor, dignity, honor, and quiet determination to do the right thing.

Ronald Reagan's presidential administration coincided with my own coming of age, and emergence from a liberal haze of ignorance and weak-minded following.

Ronald Reagan was a real American hero. An original and a role model. With his philosophical and moral guidance, we all had a chance to glimpse his shining city on a hill. Did you?

Was it a coincidence that I made the journey from a lost liberal to American conservative during President Reagan's time in office? What do you think?

35821980R00088

Made in the USA
Lexington, KY
25 September 2014